PowerShell for SQL Server Essentials

Manage and monitor SQL Server administration and application deployment with PowerShell

Donabel Santos

[PACKT] enterprise
PUBLISHING
professional expertise distilled

BIRMINGHAM - MUMBAI

PowerShell for SQL Server Essentials

Copyright © 2015 Packt Publishing

First published: February 2015

Production reference: 1200215

Published by Packt Publishing Ltd.
Livery Place
35 Livery Street
Birmingham B3 2PB, UK.

ISBN 978-1-78439-149-2

www.packtpub.com

Credits

Author
Donabel Santos

Reviewers
Mark Andrews

Peter Johnson

Rahul Singla

Acquisition Editors
Rebecca Pedley

Meeta Rajani

Content Development Editor
Akshay Nair

Technical Editors
Pragnesh Bilimoria

Taabish Khan

Copy Editors
Gladson Monteiro

Veena Mukundan

Alfida Paiva

Project Coordinator
Mary Alex

Proofreaders
Ting Baker

Simran Bhogal

Paul Hindle

Indexer
Monica Ajmera Mehta

Graphics
Valentina D'silva

Production Coordinator
Nilesh R. Mohite

Cover Work
Nilesh R. Mohite

About the Author

Donabel Santos (SQL Server MVP) is a business intelligence architect, trainer/instructor, consultant, author, and principal at QueryWorks Solutions, based in Vancouver, Canada. She works primarily with SQL Server for database/data warehouse, reporting, and ETL solutions. She scripts and automates tasks with PowerShell and creates dashboards and visualizations with Tableau and Power BI.

She is a Microsoft Certified Trainer (MCT). She provides consulting and corporate training to clients. She is also the lead instructor for SQL Server and Tableau (Visual Analytics) courses at British Columbia Institute of Technology (BCIT).

Donabel is an MCITP DBA and a developer for SQL Server and MCTS for SharePoint. She is also a Tableau Desktop 7 Core Certified and a Tableau Desktop 8 Certified Professional. She is currently working on her SQL Server 2012 (and upcoming 2014) certifications.

She is a self-confessed data geek. She loves working with data and thinks SQL Server is a lot of fun and Tableau is just amazing at delivering insights. She authored *SQL Server 2012 with PowerShell V3 Cookbook, Packt Publishing*, and contributed to *PowerShell Deep Dives, Manning Publications*. She blogs at www.sqlbelle.com and tweets at @sqlbelle.

Acknowledgments

I didn't think I had it in me to write another book. However, my niece came along after the first book was published and she wasn't in my acknowledgements. So, I wanted to have an opportunity to mention her in another book.

To my dearest Chiyo: I hope you always remember that Tita loves you very much. Tita will always be there for you whenever you need her.

In my first book, I apologized for the lengthy acknowledgements. In this second book, I will do the same.

To Eric: thank you for still being here with me through the ups and downs, the happy times, and the crazy times. I am looking forward to many more adventures, side by side, hand in hand. I love you.

To Papa and Mama: you always give me strength and inspiration. I keep on going because of you. Thank you for everything that you've done for us, and I am so happy that your granddaughter gives you a lot of joy. I love you both very much.

To JR and RR: you will always be my baby brothers, and I am so proud to be your elder sister.

To Lisa: you're my sister, and I wouldn't have it any other way. I'm there for you and will be there to support you as best as I can.

To my in laws: Mom Lisa, Dad Richard, Ama, Aunt Rose, Catherine, David, Jayden, and Kristina; thank you for being my family. Thank you for all the fun times and all the support all these years. Thank you for being there whenever I needed you; words cannot express my gratitude. Jayden and Kristina, Agim and Agu love you two very much, and we'll be there for you to play with you, teach you, and support you. We just want hugs and kisses in return.

To my BCIT family: Kevin Cudihee, Joanne Atha, Elsie Au, Cynthia van Ginkel, Steve Eccles, Dean Hildebrand, and to all my students, past and present; thank you. BCIT is my second home. It has paved the way for many good things in my life and I will always be grateful.

To my UBC family: my super wonderful boss extraordinaire, Pradeep Nair, and my superb teammates Joe Xing, Min Zhu, George Firican, Mary Mootatamby, Jason Metcalfe, Tom Yerex, and Suzanne Landry. I love going to work everyday. You are all awesome; we have a great team and it is a privilege to work with all of you.

To the Packt team: Meeta Rajani for contacting me to author this book and Akshay Nair, who has helped me throughout the process; thank you.

I didn't do this alone. I have learned so much from so many other people, all the SQL Server and PowerShell MVPs, and each technology's communities and bloggers. The Tableau community is also quite inspiring, from Zen masters (Joe Mako, Jonathan Drummey, Kelly Martin, and Dan Murray) to all the bloggers and vizzers. Special thank you to Dan Murray, Tim Costello, Jason Schumacher, John Pain, and Liz Feller. Thank you all for making learning fun again.

There are so many other people who inspired and helped me along the way, including friends, students, and acquaintances. Thank you.

Most importantly, thank you Lord for all the miracles and blessings in my life.

About the Reviewers

Mark Andrews has had a varied career in technology. Over the last 18 years, he has held several different positions, ranging from customer service to quality assurance. Throughout all these positions, the responsibility of configuration management and build management has always fallen either on Mark personally or on one of the groups that he managed. Because of his "keeping a hand in" management style, he has been involved closely with the scripting and automation framework for these areas. Creating scripted frameworks that intercommunicate across machine / operating system / domain boundaries is a passion for him.

He has worked on *PowerShell 3.0 Advanced Administration Handbook, Packt Publishing*, and *Windows PowerShell 4.0 for .NET Developers, Packt Publishing*.

Peter Johnson has over 34 years of enterprise computing experience. He started working with PowerShell when it first surfaced from Microsoft as Monad. He has been working with Java for 17 years, and for the last 12 years, he has been heavily involved in Java performance tuning. He is a frequent speaker on Java performance topics at various conferences, including the Computer Measurement Group annual conference, JBoss World, and Linux World. He is a moderator for the IDE and WildFly/JBoss forums at Java Ranch. He is also the coauthor of the book *JBoss in Action, Manning Publications*, and has been a reviewer on numerous books on topics ranging from Java to Windows PowerShell.

Rahul Singla is the founder of Imbibe Technologies Private Limited (`http://imbibe.in`), an independent software services vendor located at Karnal, India, and serves as its managing director and chief solutions architect.

Having worked with a wide spectrum of technologies and platforms, he sees technology as a means and not an end. He has helped companies, big and small, rethink their IT strategies and streamline their operations. As a developer, he has delivered solutions that work for today's enterprises and provided all sorts of integrations, ranging from payment gateways, geomapping APIs, custom COM SDKs, and a variety of cloud services.

Currently, he also serves as a senior consultant to a couple of multinational IT organizations and has previously served in similar roles for government projects and other organizations.

You can find more about him on his portal at `http://www.rahulsingla.com`. You can also find useful PowerShell-related stuff and other technical material on his blog (`http://www.rahulsingla.com/blog`). He can be contacted directly at `rs@rahulsingla.com`.

> As always, I dedicate my work first to the Almighty, who gave me the strength, perseverance, and opportunity to reach here, and then to the three most important people in my life: my father, my mother, and Rmi (my brother).

www.PacktPub.com

Support files, eBooks, discount offers, and more

For support files and downloads related to your book, please visit www.PacktPub.com.

Did you know that Packt offers eBook versions of every book published, with PDF and ePub files available? You can upgrade to the eBook version at www.PacktPub.com and as a print book customer, you are entitled to a discount on the eBook copy. Get in touch with us at service@packtpub.com for more details.

At www.PacktPub.com, you can also read a collection of free technical articles, sign up for a range of free newsletters and receive exclusive discounts and offers on Packt books and eBooks.

![PACKTLIB logo]

https://www2.packtpub.com/books/subscription/packtlib

Do you need instant solutions to your IT questions? PacktLib is Packt's online digital book library. Here, you can search, access, and read Packt's entire library of books.

Why subscribe?

- Fully searchable across every book published by Packt
- Copy and paste, print, and bookmark content
- On demand and accessible via a web browser

Free access for Packt account holders

If you have an account with Packt at www.PacktPub.com, you can use this to access PacktLib today and view 9 entirely free books. Simply use your login credentials for immediate access.

Instant updates on new Packt books

Get notified! Find out when new books are published by following @PacktEnterprise on Twitter or the *Packt Enterprise* Facebook page.

Table of Contents

Preface

PowerShell is Microsoft's platform for task automation. It comes with both a shell and scripting language, and is now more deeply integrated with Microsoft's suite of products. Microsoft applications such as Windows, Exchange, and SharePoint have increased their PowerShell support, and many tasks can now be done without having to go through the user interface. These automated and streamlined tasks equate to time savings and increased productivity for developers, administrators, and IT professionals.

As a database professional, you can also leverage PowerShell in your work. This book introduces you to PowerShell and taps into how you can use PowerShell in the context of SQL Server.

What this book covers

Chapter 1, *Getting Started with PowerShell*, introduces you to PowerShell and its importance in server management and automation. This chapter is a good starting point for readers who are new to PowerShell and want to get started with its environment and other components.

Chapter 2, *Using PowerShell with SQL Server*, dives into using SQL Server-specific PowerShell support in different operating systems and SQL Server versions. You will learn about SQL Server-specific modules, cmdlets, and SQL Management Objects (SMO).

Chapter 3, *Profiling and Configuring SQL Server*, covers how to quickly profile SQL Server and change SQL Server configurations using PowerShell. You will learn more about Get-WmiObject and the SMO Server object.

Chapter 4, Basic SQL Server Administration, covers the tasks in a DBA's checklist. These tasks include getting space/memory usage, backup/restore, enabling features, jobs, alerts, and so on.

Chapter 5, Querying SQL Server with PowerShell, shows the methods to query SQL Server from within PowerShell, its pros and cons, and how to export results.

Chapter 6, Monitoring and Automating SQL Server, teaches you how to perform SQL Server usage and performance monitoring, logging, alerting, and error checking using PowerShell.

Appendix, Implementing Reusability with Functions and Modules, shows some snippets required to accomplish the task at hand. It covers the basics of creating and deploying functions and modules.

What you need for this book

For the purpose of this book, the requirements are as follows:

- Windows Server 2012 R2 Standard
- SQL Server 2014 Developer Edition

The system requirements for Windows PowerShell 4.0 and 3.0 are as follows:

- The OS needs to be Windows 8.1, Windows Server 2012 R2, Windows 7 with Service Pack 1, Windows Server 2008 R2 with Service Pack 1, or Windows Server 2008 (for PowerShell 3.0 only)
- Microsoft .NET Framework requirements are 4.5 for PowerShell 4.0 and 4 for PowerShell 3.0
- WS-Management 3.0
- Windows Management Instrumentation 3.0
- Common Language Runtime 4.0

Who this book is for

This book is written for SQL Server administrators and developers who want to leverage PowerShell to work with SQL Server. Some background with scripting will be helpful but not necessary.

Conventions

In this book, you will find a number of text styles that distinguish between different kinds of information. Here are some examples of these styles and an explanation of their meaning.

Code words in text, database table names, folder names, filenames, file extensions, pathnames, dummy URLs, user input, and Twitter handles are shown as follows: "The -Leaf option provides the filename part of the full path."

A block of code is set as follows:

```
$server.EnumProcesses() |
Where-Object IsSystem -eq $false |
Select-Object Spid, Database |
Format-Table -AutoSize
```

When we wish to draw your attention to a particular part of a code block, the relevant lines or items are set in bold:

```
$server.EnumProcesses() |
Where-Object IsSystem -eq $false |
Select-Object Spid, Database |
Format-Table -AutoSize
```

Any command-line input or output is written as follows:

```
Get-Help Get-ChildItem -Online
```

New terms and **important words** are shown in bold. Words that you see on the screen, for example, in menus or dialog boxes, appear in the text like this: "You can click on the **CPU** or **Memory** option to sort data according to those metrics."

> Warnings or important notes appear in a box like this.

> Tips and tricks appear like this.

Reader feedback

Feedback from our readers is always welcome. Let us know what you think about this book—what you liked or disliked. Reader feedback is important for us as it helps us develop titles that you will really get the most out of.

To send us general feedback, simply e-mail feedback@packtpub.com, and mention the book's title in the subject of your message.

If there is a topic that you have expertise in and you are interested in either writing or contributing to a book, see our author guide at www.packtpub.com/authors.

Customer support

Now that you are the proud owner of a Packt book, we have a number of things to help you to get the most from your purchase.

Downloading the example code

You can download the example code files from your account at http://www. packtpub.com for all the Packt Publishing books you have purchased. If you purchased this book elsewhere, you can visit http://www.packtpub.com/support and register to have the files e-mailed directly to you.

Errata

Although we have taken every care to ensure the accuracy of our content, mistakes do happen. If you find a mistake in one of our books—maybe a mistake in the text or the code—we would be grateful if you could report this to us. By doing so, you can save other readers from frustration and help us improve subsequent versions of this book. If you find any errata, please report them by visiting http://www.packtpub.com/submit-errata, selecting your book, clicking on the **Errata Submission Form** link, and entering the details of your errata. Once your errata are verified, your submission will be accepted and the errata will be uploaded to our website or added to any list of existing errata under the Errata section of that title.

To view the previously submitted errata, go to https://www.packtpub.com/books/content/support and enter the name of the book in the search field. The required information will appear under the **Errata** section.

Piracy

Piracy of copyrighted material on the Internet is an ongoing problem across all media. At Packt, we take the protection of our copyright and licenses very seriously. If you come across any illegal copies of our works in any form on the Internet, please provide us with the location address or website name immediately so that we can pursue a remedy.

Please contact us at copyright@packtpub.com with a link to the suspected pirated material.

We appreciate your help in protecting our authors and our ability to bring you valuable content.

Questions

If you have a problem with any aspect of this book, you can contact us at questions@packtpub.com, and we will do our best to address the problem.

1
Getting Started with PowerShell

PowerShell is an object-based Microsoft scripting language that comes with its own console and GUI-based environments. PowerShell provides building blocks for automation and system integration. You can think of PowerShell as glue that can keep different Microsoft components and applications together (and make them play nicely with each other).

Knowing PowerShell can lead to power (pun intended). Treat PowerShell like a new member of your high performance team. To achieve high performance, you need to get to know PowerShell and learn its strengths before you can expect to maximize your results.

The list of topics that you will come across in this chapter is as follows:

- A brief history of PowerShell
- The PowerShell environment
- Cmdlets
- PowerShell providers
- Snap-ins and modules
- PowerShell Pipeline
- Scripting basics
- Running PowerShell scripts
- Getting help

A brief history of PowerShell

Before PowerShell, systems and network administrators managing Microsoft software stacks had to resort to using different tools, languages, and technologies to enable automation and integration tasks. For some tasks, administrators used batch files that could be run using Command Prompt (or DOS Shell, for those of you who still remember this term). For other tasks, maybe **Visual Basic Scripting Edition (VBScript)** was used. Yet, for additional tasks, maybe **Windows Scripting Host (WSH)** was used. The list goes on.

In a lot of ways, administrators had to be creative because there was not one single language and tool they could use to bridge different Microsoft (and non-Microsoft) tasks together. Unix and Linux administrators, on the other hand, always had C-shell and trusty bash to rely on. At that time, Microsoft just did not have that powerful a command-line tool.

Enter PowerShell. PowerShell was born out of this need for integration and automation. Jeffrey Snover, the inventor of PowerShell, initially incubated PowerShell under the project named Monad. He originally described Monad as the *next generation platform for automation*.

> You can read the Monad Manifesto written by Jeffrey Snover in 2002 at http://www.jsnover.com/Docs/MonadManifesto.pdf.

More than 10 years after this manifesto was written, PowerShell has already improved and matured in leaps and bounds and has indeed become the platform for automation and integration for Microsoft products (and even non-Microsoft packages).

As of today, many Microsoft products have adopted PowerShell and delivered numerous cmdlets (we will talk about them later) with their respective product installations. Windows Server, Active Directory, Exchange, SharePoint, SQL Server are products that support PowerShell (to different extents), but the support has widened through the years.

The PowerShell environment

There are two environments that come with PowerShell when you install it: the PowerShell console and the **PowerShell Integrated Scripting Environment** (**ISE**). These environments have improved a lot since the first version and should be more than sufficient for you to start working with PowerShell. If you prefer a different environment, there are other PowerShell editors out there. Some editors are free and some commercial. Some vendors that provide PowerShell editors are Idera (PowerShell Plus), Dell (PowerGUI), and SAPIEN Technologies (PowerShell Studio 2014).

> This book uses the current released version at the time of writing, which is PowerShell v4. The screenshots you will see in this book reflect the screens in PowerShell v4.

In a 64-bit system, PowerShell will come in two flavors: 32 bit and 64 bit. The 32-bit version has the label suffix **(x86)**. Note that 64-bit add-ons and snap-ins for PowerShell will only load in the 64-bit console or ISE. The following screenshot shows the result of searching PowerShell in Windows:

The PowerShell console

The PowerShell console is very similar to the Command Prompt. By default, the interface is blue, compared to the usual black of the Command Prompt:

The PowerShell console is great for administrators and IT professionals who prefer to work on a purely command-line environment. The console is also great for running predefined scripts either manually or through a job via the Windows task scheduler or SQL Server Agent.

The PowerShell ISE

A standard installation of PowerShell also comes with an **Integrated Scripting Environment (ISE)**. The PowerShell ISE is a more **Graphical User Interface (GUI)** way of working with PowerShell and comes with a few handy features, including IntelliSense and syntax help, as shown in the following screenshot:

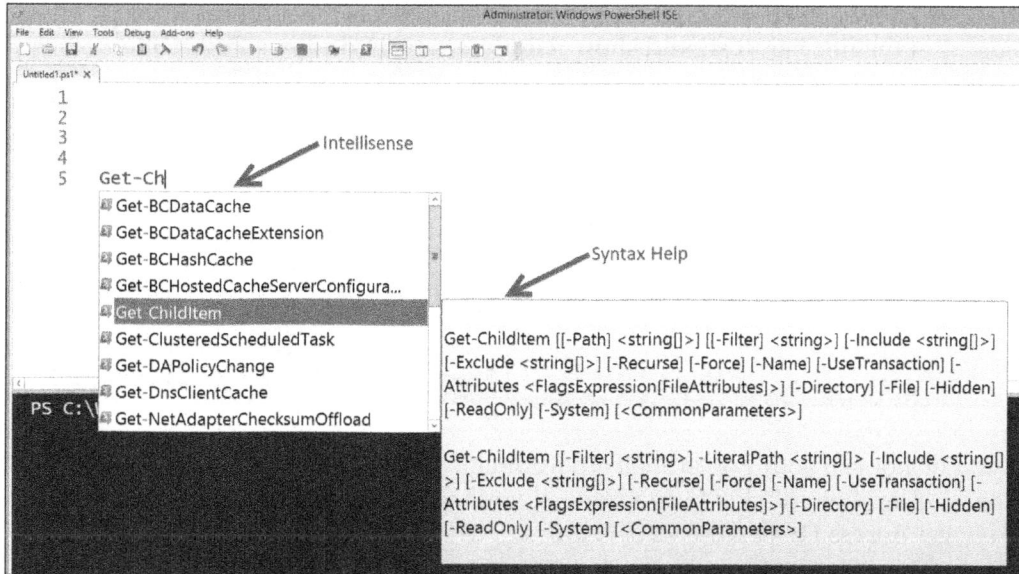

Some of the compelling features that the ISE has are listed as follows:

- The script editor and PowerShell console in a single environment
- The autocomplete and on-hover usage/syntax guide
- A command pane that allows you to visually fill in parameters and transfer the syntax over to your editor
- Multiple tabs that allows the opening of multiple scripts at the same time
- A zoom slider, which is great for presentations or just basic readability

We will use the PowerShell ISE for most examples in this book.

Running PowerShell as an administrator

Most of the time, you will use PowerShell to perform administrative tasks, so you will need to run it as an administrator. You can do this by right-clicking on the application (console or ISE) and clicking on **Run as administrator**.

You will know you've successfully run the application as the administrator by looking at the title bar. It should show **Administrator: Windows PowerShell**:

```
Administrator: Windows PowerShell
PS C:\Users\Administrator.QUERYWORKS> Get-Help Get-Service

NAME
    Get-Service

SYNOPSIS
    Gets the services on a local or remote computer.
```

If you do not run your PowerShell environment as the administrator, you might not have sufficient permission to run some of your commands or scripts. You will most likely get **Access Denied** errors.

A useful trick to identify whether you are running the shell as the administrator is to change the appearance of the shell based on the elevation status of the session. This can be accomplished by adding a snippet of code to your profile that checks whether the session is run by an administrator and then changing some properties accordingly.

First you need to check whether your profile exists. You can check the path to your profile by typing the following command:

```
$profile
```

If this file doesn't exist, you can simply create it by typing the following:

```
New-Item -ItemType File $profile -Force
```

The $profile command is equivalent to $profile.CurrentUserCurrentHost, which means the settings you provided will only work on the current host. Note that your console and ISE will each have its own profile, so you may need to create one for each. The values you can specify with the profile are AllUUsersAllHosts, AllUsersCurrentHost, CurrentUserAllHosts, and CurrentUserCurrentHost.

Here is a simple snippet you can add to your profile that changes the background and foreground color of your shell if you running the shell as an administrator:

```
if ($host.UI.RawUI.WindowTitle -match "Administrator")
{
    $host.UI.RawUI.BackgroundColor = "DarkRed"
    $host.UI.RawUI.ForegroundColor = "White"
}
```

The execution policy

At the risk of sounding like a dictionary, I will define execution policy as the policy applied to determine whether a script can be executed by PowerShell. Execution policies do not make the scripts more secure. They simply lay the ground rules before a script is executed.

The available execution policies are provided in the following table:

Policy	Runs a command?	Runs a local script?	Runs a remote script?
Restricted	Yes	No	No
AllSigned	Yes	Must be signed	Must be signed
RemoteSigned	Yes	Yes	Must be signed
Unrestricted	Yes	Yes	Yes – prompts before running downloaded scripts
Bypass	Yes	Yes	Yes – no warnings or prompts

The default execution policy depends on the operating system you are using. For Windows 8, Windows Server 2012, and Windows 8.1, the default policy is Restricted. For Windows Server 2012 R2, it is RemoteSigned.

Should you need to sign your scripts, you can refer to Scott Hanselman's blog post available at http://www.hanselman.com/blog/SigningPowerShellScripts. aspx. Although this was written a few years ago, the content is still relevant. Patrick Fegan from Risual also has a good, more recent tutorial on self-signing PowerShell scripts at http://consulting.risualblogs.com/blog/2013/09/20/signing-powershell-scripts/.

> To get more information about execution policies, including risks and suggestions on how to manage them, you can type Get-Help about_Execution_Policies in the command-line window, or you can visit the TechNet page at http://technet.microsoft.com/en-us/library/hh847748.aspx for more detailed descriptions.

If you want to check which execution policy you are running on, you can use the following command:

```
Get-ExecutionPolicy
```

If you want to change it, use the following command:

```
Set-ExecutionPolicy
```

The following is a screenshot of what you can expect when you run these two cmdlets:

```
Administrator: Windows PowerShell                              _ □ X

PS C:\> Get-ExecutionPolicy
RemoteSigned
PS C:\> Set-ExecutionPolicy Unrestricted

Execution Policy Change
The execution policy helps protect you from scripts that you do not trust.
Changing the execution policy might expose you to the security risks described
in the about_Execution_Policies help topic at
http://go.microsoft.com/fwlink/?LinkID=135170. Do you want to change the
execution policy?
[Y] Yes  [N] No  [S] Suspend  [?] Help (default is "Y"): Y
PS C:\> _
```

It would be good to read more on execution policies, evaluate the risks that come with the different settings, and evaluate your needs before deciding which setting you should use.

PowerShell versions

PowerShell has matured since its inception and has undergone several version upgrades. At the time of writing of this book, the most recent version is PowerShell V4.

The following table shows the different PowerShell versions that Microsoft released, operating systems that support them, required .NET Framework version, and some of the notable features:

PowerShell version	OS support	.NET version	Notable features/additions
Version 1, which is a separate download	Windows XP, Windows Server 2003, and Windows Vista	.NET Framework 2.0	Over 130 cmdlets

PowerShell version	OS support	.NET version	Notable features/additions
Version 2, which is part of WMF 2.0	• Integrated with Windows 7 and Windows Server 2008 R2 • Available for XP and Windows Server 2003 • Can be downloaded separately as part of WMF 2.0	.NET Framework 2.0 or .NET Framework 3.5 SP1	Over 240 cmdlets, which includes PowerShell ISE, remoting, eventing, background jobs, script debugging, and modules
Version 3, which is part of WMF 3.0	• Integrated with Windows 8 and Windows Server 2012 • Available for 7 and Windows Server 2008 and later	.NET Framework 4.0 full	• Over 400 cmdlets • Workflows, improved sessions, scheduled jobs, and the `Update-Help` cmdlet • PowerShell ISE improvements, which include IntelliSense, command pane, and collapsible regions
Version 4, which is part of WMF 4.0	• Integrated with Windows 8.1 and Windows Server 2012 R2 • Available for Windows 7 and Windows Server 2008 and later	.NET Framework 4.5 full	• Over 520 cmdlets • Desired state configuration • Shell and scripting improvements
Version 5, which is part of WMF 5.0	At the time of writing this, a CTP version is available with Windows Management Framework 5.0	NA	NA

PowerShell matures with every release and the requirements and features will change with different operating systems.

> Please visit `http://technet.microsoft.com/en-us/library/hh847769.aspx` for official PowerShell requirements required for your Windows OS.

To determine which PowerShell version you are using, you can type in `$PSVersionTable` in your console or ISE:

If you have PowerShell v3 or v4, you can also *downgrade* your PowerShell session. You can do this by supplying the `-Version` parameter when you start your session:

```
Powershell.exe -Version 2
```

PowerShell cmdlets

At the heart of PowerShell is a cmdlet (pronounced as commandlet). A cmdlet is described in MSDN (available at `http://msdn.microsoft.com/en-us/library/ms714395(v=vs.85).aspx`) as:

> *"… a lightweight command that is used in the Windows PowerShell environment.*
>
> *… cmdlets perform an action and typically return a Microsoft .NET Framework object to the next command in the pipeline."*

In other words, cmdlets get the job done in PowerShell. You can think of cmdlets as *small commands* — very specific commands — which you can use to accomplish your task.

To explore the cmdlets available in your PowerShell version, you can use the `Get-Command` cmdlet. You can filter the results as well. For example, if you want to look for log-related cmdlets, you can use the following command:

```
Get-Command -Name "*Log*"
```

Cmdlet naming convention

Cmdlets have a very specific naming convention. They follow the `Verb-Noun` format and they are typically self-explanatory. More specifically, it is `Verb-SingularNoun`.

The following are some example cmdlets available in PowerShell:

- `Get-Service`
- `Test-Path`
- `Set-Content`
- `ConvertTo-Csv`

Note that cmdlet names are self-documenting. You don't really have to guess what the `Get-Service` cmdlet does; it gets the corresponding services in your system.

You can get a list of legal, endorsed verbs by Microsoft using the `Get-Verb` cmdlet. Granted, not all the terms you see are really verbs, but for our purposes, we will treat them as such. For example, Microsoft uses the `New` verb to create new items:

- `New-Service`
- `New-Event`
- `New-Object`

Another verb that Microsoft considers is `Out`, mostly used for output. Take a look at the following examples:

- `Out-File`
- `Out-GridView`
- `Out-Null`

Cmdlet parameters

Note that cmdlets can accept parameters or switches. This makes cmdlets quite flexible. You can supply parameters to cmdlets by specifying a dash followed by a parameter name, space, and the parameter value:

```
Cmdlet -ParameterName ParameterValue -ParameterName ParameterValue
```

It will be easier to understand how parameters work if we go through an example. Let's take a look at the usage syntax for Get-Service:

```
Administrator: Windows PowerShell
PS C:\Users\Administrator.QUERYWORKS> Get-Help Get-Service

NAME
    Get-Service

SYNOPSIS
    Gets the services on a local or remote computer.


SYNTAX
    Get-Service [[-Name] <String[]>] [-ComputerName <String[]>]
    [-DependentServices] [-Exclude <String[]>] [-Include <String[]>]
    [-RequiredServices] [<CommonParameters>]

    Get-Service [-ComputerName <String[]>] [-DependentServices] [-Exclude
    <String[]>] [-Include <String[]>] [-RequiredServices] -DisplayName
    <String[]> [<CommonParameters>]

    Get-Service [-ComputerName <String[]>] [-DependentServices] [-Exclude
    <String[]>] [-Include <String[]>] [-InputObject <ServiceController[]>]
    [-RequiredServices] [<CommonParameters>]
```

Each block in the help section, shown in the preceding screenshot, represents a parameter set. Each parameter set specifies different combinations of parameters and switches that are all valid when you use Get-Service.

> Anything in square brackets is optional; anything between angle brackets is mandatory.

Let's consider the following first line of command:

```
Get-Service [[-Name] <String[]>] [-ComputerName <String[]>]
```

The `[[-Name] <String[]>]` part means that you can specify `-Name`, which should be your parameter name:

```
Get-Service -Name *SQL*
```

Since `[[-Name] <String[]>]` is surrounded by square brackets, it means it's optional. This parameter name can be left out and you can provide just the value. This makes it positional, meaning the value you provide will map to the parameter defined for that cmdlet at that position. In the following example, the first value will be mapped to the first parameter for `Get-Service`:

```
Get-Service *SQL*
```

The next part `[-ComputerName <String[]>]` is still overall an optional parameter. However, if you decide to supply the value, you have to specify the parameter name, which is `ComputerName`. Note that there is no square bracket around `ComputerName`.

When you specify parameter names, you can also take shortcuts. You can specify just the first few characters of the parameter name, and as long as it's unique, PowerShell will figure out which parameter you are referring to:

```
Get-Service -Na *SQL*
```

> Although it's quite tempting to use shortcuts, when you are first learning how to use PowerShell, try to always completely spell out the parameter names. This will make your code more readable and easier for the rest of your team to work with your code.

If you have a cmdlet that requires input and you don't provide it, you will be prompted for the values interactively:

```
Administrator: Windows PowerShell
PS C:\Users\Administrator.QUERYWORKS> Restart-Service

cmdlet Restart-Service at command pipeline position 1
Supply values for the following parameters:
InputObject[0]:
```

Cmdlet aliases

Some of the cmdlets also have aliases by default. This means these cmdlets can be invoked by using a different name than their formal cmdlet name. For example, the following screenshot shows the aliases for Get-ChildItem:

You can also create your own aliases using New-Alias. Aliases can be useful because in some ways, they allow you to use some of the terms you may already be familiar with and leverage them in PowerShell. Aliases also let you personalize PowerShell to your liking. Be careful not to create too many of these though; it may make your PowerShell scripts confusing and even unreadable to others.

PowerShell providers

Simply put, a PowerShell provider *provides* a way for PowerShell to access a data store. To get a visual of a provider, think of the file system. The file system is a data store that contains information about files and folders and their properties. We can access the file system via the Command Prompt, PowerShell console, or Windows Explorer. Now try to apply this concept to another data store, for example, SQL Server. Imagine that you can navigate through the objects of SQL Server just the way you navigate your file system.

Learning about providers is important because this allows you to extend what you can do with PowerShell. To list the current providers in your system, use the Get-PSProvider cmdlet:

```
Administrator: Windows PowerShell
PS C:\Users\Administrator.QUERYWORKS> Get-PSProvider

Name                    Capabilities
----                    ------------
Alias                   ShouldProcess
Environment             ShouldProcess
FileSystem              Filter, ShouldProcess, Credentials
Function                ShouldProcess
Registry                ShouldProcess, Transactions
Variable                ShouldProcess
```

What you see in the preceding screenshot are the default available providers that come with PowerShell v4 on a Windows Server 2012 R2 Standard server. A lot of the providers are accessed using what is called drives. To list the current drives, you can use `Get-PSDrive`:

```
Administrator: Windows PowerShell
PS C:\Users\Administrator.QUERYWORKS> Get-PSDrive

Name        Used (GB)    Free (GB) Provider      Root
----        ---------    --------- --------      ----
A                                  FileSystem    A:\
Alias                              Alias
C               20.10       99.90  FileSystem    C:\
Cert                               Certificate   \
D                3.63              FileSystem    D:\
Env                                Environment
Function                           Function
HKCU                               Registry      HKEY_CURRENT_USER
HKLM                               Registry      HKEY_LOCAL_MACHINE
Variable                           Variable
WSMan                              WSMan
```

In a file system, if you wanted to change drives, you can use the `cd` command, which is an alias for `Set-Location`:

```
C:\> cd J:\
```

To navigate to a different provider, you can use the same concept. For example, if you want to navigate the HKLM registry hive (which stands for HKEY_LOCAL_MACHINE), you can use the following command lines:

```
C:\> cd HKLM:
HKLM:\>
```

To work with items in `PSDrive`, Microsoft has provided a number of `Item` cmdlets that are generic enough to perform the task regardless of which drive you are in. To get a list of these cmdlets, you can type `Get-Command *Item*`. For example, if you are using a file system, you can use the `New-Item` cmdlet to create a new folder or file. If you are in the registry, it will create a new registry entry.

The recent releases of Microsoft products come with their own PowerShell providers, which you can readily use. You can also create your own providers if you prefer.

> MSDN has some documentation on how you can create your own provider available at `http://msdn.microsoft.com/en-us/library/ee126192(v=vs.85).aspx`. There are even tutorials on how to create providers for non-Microsoft data stores. For example, the version control system Git by @manojlds is available at `http://stacktoheap.com/blog/2012/12/01/writing-a-git-provider-for-windows-powershell-part-1/`.

Snap-ins and modules

You can extend PowerShell by loading snap-ins and modules. Snap-ins or `PSSnapins` are **dynamic linked library (DLLs)** compiled from .NET code, which may contain additional cmdlets and `PSProvider`. The `PSSnapins` are *old school*—they are primarily how you extend version 1, but still supported in version 2, version 3, and version 4. Although considered old school, you can still create snap-ins. Refer to `http://msdn.microsoft.com/en-us/library/ms714450(v=vs.85).aspx` on how to do this.

The related snap-in cmdlets are as follows:

* `Add-PSSnapin`
* `Get-PSSnapin`
* `Remove-PSSnapin`

Instead of snap-ins, the recommended way of extending the PowerShell functionality from version 2 onwards is using modules. Modules are similar to snap-ins when it comes to extending functionality, but unlike snap-ins, modules can also add functions. Modules also support autoloading, which means the module can be loaded as soon as one of its cmdlets/functions/`PSDrive` are used.

Modules can be script-based or binary-based. A script module uses PowerShell code saved in a `.psm1` file. A binary module is more similar to `PSSnapin`, where it references a .NET DLL.

Modules are the *new school* way of extending PowerShell, from version 2 onwards. Related cmdlets are listed as follows:

- `Import-Module`
- `Get-Module`
- `Remove-Module`

If you want to write PowerShell extensions, Microsoft recommends that you create modules instead of snap-ins.

PowerShell Pipeline

A pipeline is defined in `www.TheFreeDictionary.com` as follows:

> *"a linked series of pipes with pumps and valves for flow control, used to transport crude oil, water, etc., esp. over great distances."*

I think this definition is very fitting to a pipeline in PowerShell. Instead of crude oil or water, what PowerShell transports is pieces of information. PowerShell also has these *pumps and valves for flow control* — we will see more of these in the later chapters.

The pipe symbol in PowerShell is |, also called a bar. You can pipe multiple cmdlets together. When you pipe these cmdlets, the output of one cmdlet becomes the input of the next cmdlet:

```
Get-Service | Select-Object ServiceName, Status | Sort-Object Status -Descending
```

When you are writing your scripts, you may want to add a new line after the pipe and continue typing the next cmdlet on the new line:

```
Get-Service |
Select-Object ServiceName, Status |
Sort-Object Status -Descending
```

Many script authors also prefer to indent the succeeding lines a little bit to emphasize that these are all part of the same block.

Scripting basics

Let's get a few syntax basics down. This section is not meant to be an exhaustive tutorial on PowerShell's syntax but should serve as a good, brief introduction.

Let's walk through the following script:

```
$currdate = (Get-Date -Format "yyyyMMdd hhmmtt")
$servers = @("ROGUE", "CEREBRO")


#save each server's running services into a file
$servers   |
ForEach-Object {

    $computername = $_
    Write-Host "`n`nProcessing $computername"

    $filename = "C:\Temp\$($computername) - $($currdate).csv"

    Get-Service -ComputerName $computername |
    Where-Object -Property Status -EQ "Running" |
    Select-Object Name, DisplayName |
    Export-Csv -Path $filename -NoTypeInformation


}
```

Even if you are not very familiar with PowerShell yet, you may already be able to tell what the preceding script is trying to accomplish. Simply put, the script iterates over the listed servers and saves the list of running services into a file that acts as a timestamp.

This line creates a variable called $currdate that gets the current system date in the "yyyyMMdd hhmmtt" format:

```
$currdate = (Get-Date -Format "yyyyMMdd hhmmtt")
```

The snippet with an at (@) sign, @("ROGUE", "CEREBRO"), creates an array, which is then stored in another variable called $servers:

```
$servers = @("ROGUE", "CEREBRO")
```

Since `$servers` contains multiple values, when you pipe it to the `Foreach-Object` cmdlet, each value is fed into the script block inside `Foreach-Object`:

```
#save each server's running services into a file
$servers    |
ForEach-Object {


}
```

You are also introduced to a few concepts inside the `Foreach-Object` block.

To get the current pipeline object, you can use `$_`. The `$_`, also referred to as `$PSItem`, is a special variable. It is part of what PowerShell calls automatic variables. This variable only exists and can only be used in the content of a pipeline. The `$_` variable contains the current object in the pipeline, allowing you to perform specific actions on it during the iteration:

```
$computername = $_
```

A backtick is an escape character, for example, to add a newline. It is also a line continuation character:

```
Write-Host "`n`nProcessing $computername"
```

Note that the strings are enclosed in double quotes:

```
Write-Host "`n`nProcessing $computername"
```

Strings in PowerShell can also be enclosed in single quotes. However, if you have variables you want to be evaluated within the string, as in the preceding example, you will have to use double quotes. Single quotes will simply output the variable name verbatim.

PowerShell has a subexpression operator, `$()`. This allows you to embed another variable or expression inside a string in double quotes, and PowerShell will still extract the variable value or evaluate the expression:

```
$filename = "C:\Temp\$($computername) - $($currdate).csv"
```

Here is another example that demonstrates when subexpressions will be useful. The expression to get the date that is 10 days from today is as follows:

```
(Get-Date).AddDays(10)
```

If we want to display the value this expression returns, you may be tempted to use:

```
Write-Host "10 days from now is (Get-Date).AddDays(10)"
```

However, this simply redisplays the expression; it doesn't evaluate it. One way to get around this without using a subexpression would be to create a new variable and then use it in the double-quoted string:

```
$currdate = (Get-Date).AddDays(10)
Write-Host "10 days from now is $currdate"
```

With the subexpression, you don't need to create the new variable:

```
Write-Host "10 days from now is $((Get-Date).AddDays(10))"
```

The example we walked through should give you a taste of simple scripting in PowerShell.

The following is a table that outlines some of these common scripting components and operators:

Component	Symbol	Description/examples
Single line comment	#	This component allows you to include any comments or documentation about your code; text after # in a line is not executed, for example, #get the current date.

Multiline comment	<# #>	This allows you to create comments that span multiple lines, as shown in the following example:
		
		``
		<#
		  get the current
		  date
		#>
		``

Backtick	`	Backtick can be used as an escape character: ```$name = "Hello `n world!"``` This is also a line continuation character; it allows you to break a command into multiple lines — some find it more readable, but beware that some will find it less readable because the backtick character can be conspicuous: ``` Get-Service `     -Name *SQL* ` -ComputerName ROGUE ```
Dollar sign	$	By default, variables in PowerShell are loosely typed (that is, the data type changes based on the value stored by the variable): ```$dt = Get-Date```
Single quotes	'	This component allows you to enclose string literals: ```$name = 'sqlbelle'```

Component	Symbol	Description/examples

Double quotes	"	This component allows you to enclose string literals:
		
		`$name = "sqlbelle"`
		
		This component also allows you to expand variables (that is, replace variable names within the string to their values) or interpret escape characters:
		
		`$name = "sqlbelle"`
		`$message = "Hello `n $name"`

Plus	+	This component is a string concatenation operator:
		
		`$name = "sqlbelle"`
		`$message = "Hello " + $name`

Dot	.	This component allows you to access properties or methods with the corresponding object: `$dt.AddDays(10)`
Subexpression	$()	This component allows you to embed a variable or expression in a double-quoted string; PowerShell evaluates the expression inside this operator: `Write-Host "Date: $($dt.AddDays(10))"`
At sign	@()	This component is an array subexpression operator: `@("ROGUE", "CEREBRO")`

Square brackets	[]	This component is an index operator. It allows you to access indexed collections (arrays and hash tables):
		
		`$servers = @("ROGUE", "CEREBRO")`
		`$servers[0]`
		
		It also acts as a casting operator:
		
		`[datetime] $dt`

Here-String	@"
	"@
		This component allows you to create a multiline string to assign to a variable without having to break the string into multiple string expressions concatenated by a plus (+) sign. It starts with @" and must end with "@ in a line by itself (no characters or spaces before ending "@):
		
		`$x = "@`
		`Hello $name.`
		`This is a multiline`
		`string`
		`"@`

The table is not a comprehensive list of operators or syntax about PowerShell. As you learn more about PowerShell, you will find a lot of additional components and different variations from what has been presented here.

> To learn more about operators, use `Get-Help *Operator*` and go through all the available topics. You can also go to the TechNet page specifically for operators, which is available at `http://technet.microsoft.com/en-us/library/hh847732.aspx`.

Running PowerShell scripts

Once you've written your script, save your script in a file with a `.ps1` extension. From the PowerShell console, you can run the script by specifying the full path to the script:

```
PS C:\> C:\Scripts\Get-RunningServices.ps1
```

Note that your scripts can also be parameterized so that it can take an incoming value when invoked. If this is the case, you can specify the parameter the same way you specify it in a regular cmdlet:

```
PS C:\> C:\Scripts\Get-RunningServices.ps1 -ComputerName ROGUE
```

If you are at the script directory, you don't have to specify the path. You can also use a dot-sourcing operator to run the script. Dot sourcing a script means that any of the variables and functions in the script are loaded into the current scope and available for use in the same console session:

```
PS C:\Scripts> .\Get-RunningServices.ps1
PS C:\Scripts> .\Get-RunningServices.ps1 -ComputerName ROGUE
```

Note that depending on your execution policy settings, the script may run or get access denied errors. If this is the case, you may either need to adjust your execution policy or sign your script.

Getting help

PowerShell used to come bundled with help documentation. If you've worked with *nix systems, it's similar to the man page.

Starting with PowerShell v3, however, the help files/system were not installed with PowerShell. One of the chronic problems with a help system that comes bundled with an application is that the contents get outdated right away. Applications are continuously being patched, improved, and changed, and thus the documentation needs to be updated. You will need to consciously download and install the help files when you are ready.

Once ready, run PowerShell as an administrator and just type in the following command:

```
Update-Help
```

This will connect you to a Microsoft server to download the most recent version of PowerShell help:

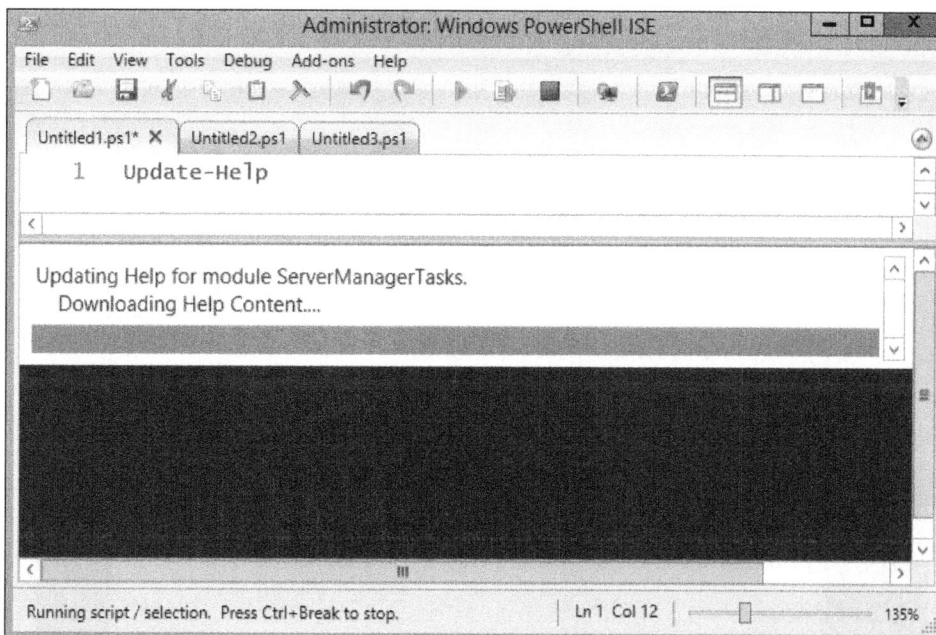

When you need to look for syntaxes or examples from the help system, you can use `Get-Help` and then the cmdlet name. For example, if you want to get `ChildItem`, you can use the following command:

```
Get-Help Get-ChildItem
```

Other switches available for `Get-Help` that you might find useful are as follows:

- `Get-Help Get-ChildItem -Detailed`
- `Get-Help Get-ChildItem -Examples`
- `Get-Help Get-ChildItem -Full`

> `Get-Help` can also be simply referred to as help.

Sometimes you may prefer to open the local help system in a different window, in which case you can use the following command:

```
Get-Help Get-ChildItem -ShowWindow
```

The result is shown in the following screenshot:

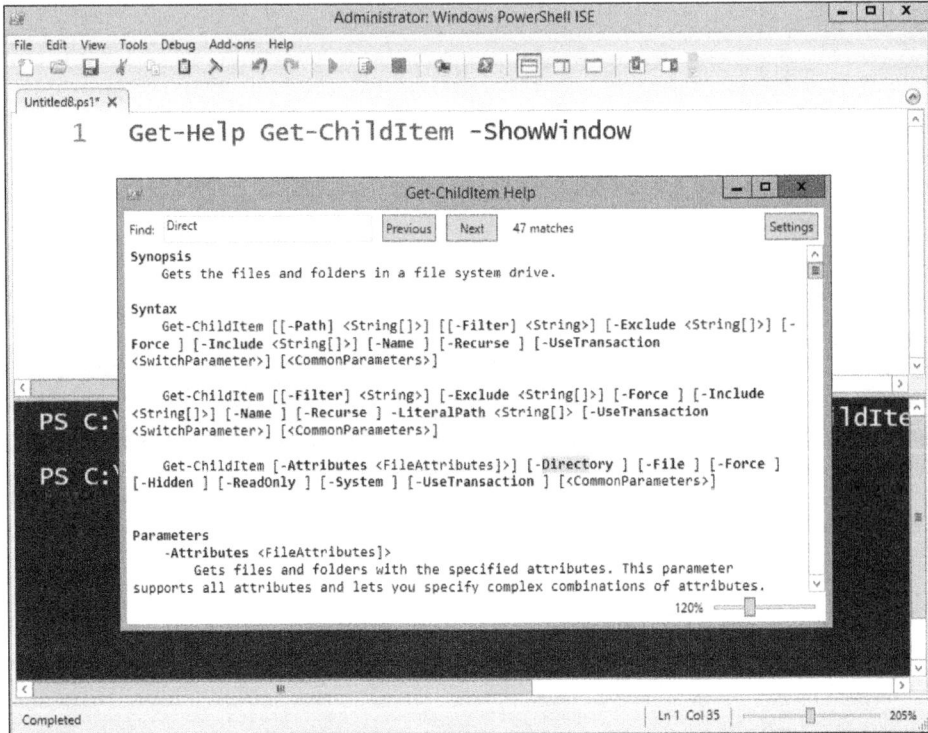

Having the help document in a different window allows you to do simultaneous tasks, that is, write your script and refer to the syntaxes and examples. The help window also allows for searching and highlighting keywords.

If what you prefer is to view the help online and get the most recent version to date, you can use the following command instead:

```
Get-Help Get-ChildItem -Online
```

This will open the corresponding Microsoft TechNet entry in your default browser:

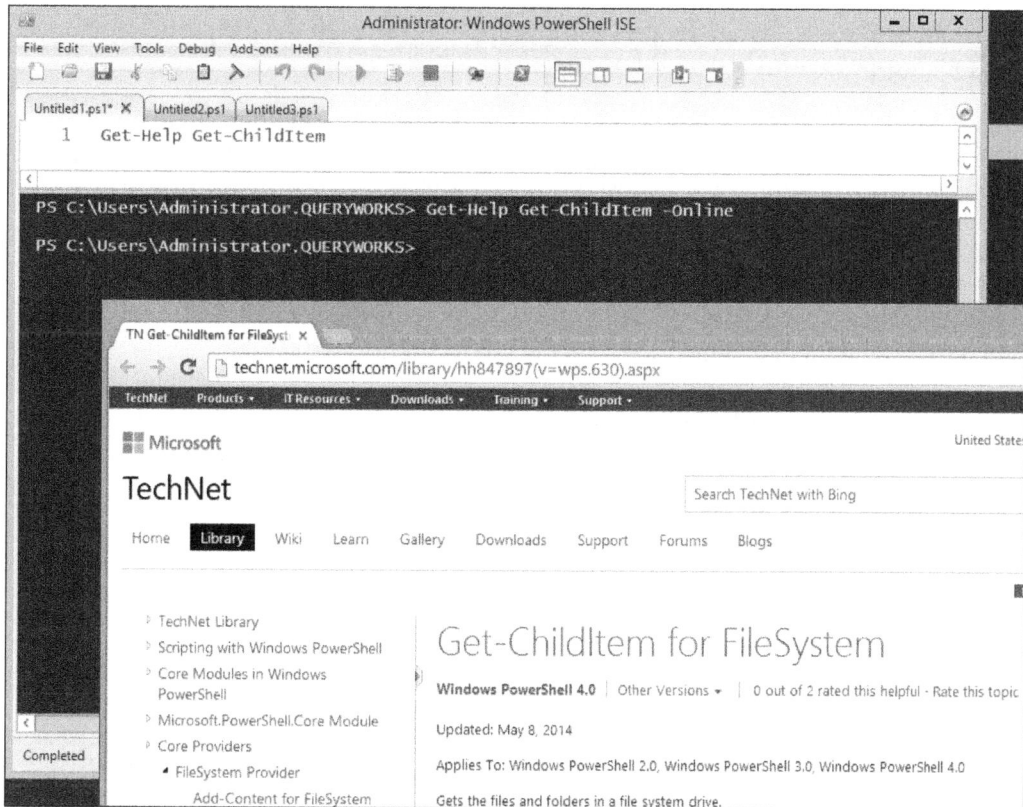

Getting help from other cmdlets

In addition to `Get-Help`, there are two other trusty cmdlets you should know if you want to know PowerShell a lot better. If you need to use a command but only remember the name or part of the name or if you want to get a list of commands based on parameters, you can use `Get-Command`. For example, as introduced earlier in the chapter, you can get log-related cmdlets using the following command:

```
Get-Command -Name "*Log*"
```

If you need to know what properties and methods are available for an object—for example, a variable or the result returned by a cmdlet—you can use `Get-Member`, as shown in the following example:

```
$message = "Hello World!"
$message | Get-Member
```

Since a message is a string, the preceding snippet returns all the properties and methods supported for a string data type.

Two risk-mitigation parameters that you should also get acquainted with are `-WhatIf` and `-Confirm`. You can add these two parameters to most cmdlets, and they can help you avoid really stressful "oops" situations.

The `-WhatIf` parameter describes the effect of a command instead of executing it. The `-Confirm` parameter forces a prompt before executing the command. It pays to be careful before you run scripts in your environment. It pays to be extra careful; as much as possible, test your scripts in a test environment first.

Downloading the example code

You can download the example code files for all Packt books you have purchased from your account at `http://www.packtpub.com`. If you purchased this book elsewhere, you can visit `http://www.packtpub.com/support` and register to have the files e-mailed directly to you.

Summary

This chapter has provided a very basic introduction to PowerShell, from a brief history to environments, cmdlets, and pipelines. This should be enough to get you familiarized with PowerShell fundamentals, a skill you will need to work with the next chapters. It is also important to remember how you can learn more about PowerShell using cmdlets such as `Get-Help`, `Get-Command`, and `Get-Member`. The more comfortable you are looking for resources on your own, the faster and better it will be for you when it comes to learning PowerShell.

This chapter is not meant to be an exhaustive, one-stop shop for PowerShell. There are a number of excellent PowerShell books out there that dig deeper into PowerShell's technicalities, syntaxes, and advanced features.

In the next chapter, we will look at how PowerShell can be integrated with SQL Server.

2
Using PowerShell with SQL Server

A number of Microsoft applications have increased their PowerShell support with each new release. Enterprise applications, such as Microsoft Windows Server, Exchange, SharePoint, and SQL Server, all have PowerShell support through cmdlets and providers that come with their default installations. Even cloud solutions, such as Windows Azure, have PowerShell support.

In this chapter, we will specifically look at components and pre-requisites required for working with SQL Server using PowerShell. Before you run the scripts in this chapter, remember to run your PowerShell console or ISE as an administrator and set the execution policy to the appropriate one in your environment. The topics included in the chapter are as follows:

- Mini-shell (or the `sqlps` utility)
- SQLPS module
- SQL Server snap-ins
- SQL Server assemblies
- SQL Server-specific cmdlets
- SQL **Server Management Objects (SMO)**

SQL Server via PowerShell

There are several ways to work with SQL Server via PowerShell. The way you choose to work will largely depend not only on what version of SQL Server and PowerShell you have, but also on what you want to do with SQL Server.

Mini-shell (or the sqlps utility)

Starting from SQL Server 2008, SQL Server was shipped with what used to be called a mini-shell (the `sqlps` utility). Back then, the mini-shell was a *limited* PowerShell console specifically bundled with SQL Server, which preloaded the `sqlps` utility, which in turn preloaded the session with the SQL Server PowerShell providers and cmdlets.

The mini-shell can be invoked in a couple of ways. One way is to go to **SQL Server Management Studio (SSMS)** and right-click on a SQL Server object and choose **Start PowerShell**. The following screenshot shows what you will see on a SQL Server 2014 interface, which is not that different from what you will see in SQL Server 2008, SQL Server 2008 R2, and SQL Server 2012:

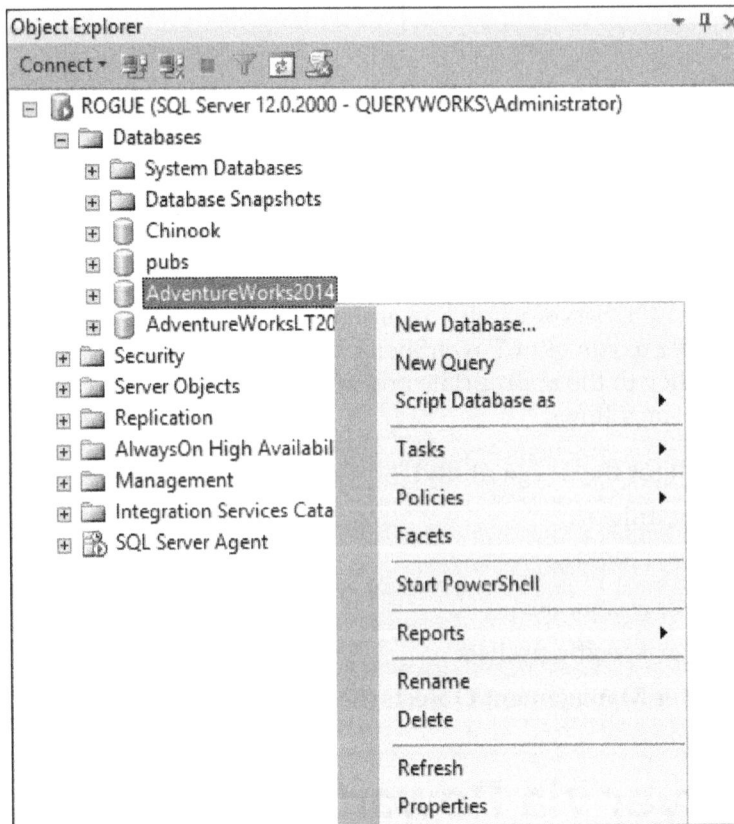

Once you click on the **Start PowerShell** option, you will see a new PowerShell console window appear. The starting path of the console will be the node you right-clicked on, so the path will change based on where you invoked the mini-shell. In the following screenshot, notice that the starting path is **AdventureWorks2014**. This indicates that we right-clicked on the AdventureWorks2014 database in SQL Server Management Studio when we launched PowerShell:

```
                          SQL Server Powershell
PS SQLSERVER:\SQL\ROGUE\DEFAULT\Databases\AdventureWorks2014> dir
ApplicationRoles
Assemblies
AsymmetricKeys
Certificates
DatabaseAuditSpecifications
Defaults
ExtendedProperties
ExtendedStoredProcedures
Federations
FileGroups
FullTextCatalogs
FullTextStopLists
LogFiles
PartitionFunctions
PartitionSchemes
PlanGuides
Roles
Rules
Schemas
```

When the mini-shell is open, you can start navigating and working with SQL Server objects using commands that you may already be familiar with, such as `dir` to list the current directory. The `dir` command is an alias for the `Get-ChildItem` cmdlet. Prior to SQL Server 2012, mini-shell used a PowerShell v1 shell and did not allow the loading of any other extensions such as snap-ins and other .NET assemblies. This restricted what you can do with that console and session.

Starting from SQL Server 2012, your system's current PowerShell version is loaded and the restriction of adding additional snap-ins and modules have been lifted. Note that Microsoft recommends that you don't use the `sqlps` utility anymore, as this is slated to be removed in a future SQL Server version. Instead of the `sqlps` utility, the newer, improved SQLPS module should be used. You can load this module from a full PowerShell console.

> Learn more about the sqlps utility, including supported parameters, examples, and associated DLLs, from TechNet at `http://msdn.microsoft.com/en-us/library/cc280450(v=sql.120).aspx`.

To see which version of PowerShell your mini-shell is using, you can use the `$PSVersionTable` special PowerShell variable:

```
SQL Server Powershell                                        _ □ X

PS SQLSERVER:\SQL\ROGUE\DEFAULT\Databases\AdventureWorks2014\tables> $PSVersionT
able

Name                          Value
----                          -----
PSVersion                     4.0
WSManStackVersion             3.0
SerializationVersion          1.1.0.1
CLRVersion                    4.0.30319.34014
BuildVersion                  6.3.9600.17090
PSCompatibleVersions          {1.0, 2.0, 3.0, 4.0}
PSRemotingProtocolVersion     2.2
```

The SQLPS module

The way to interact with SQL Server has been redefined in SQL Server 2012. Instead of using the `sqlps` utility, a SQLPS module has been made available. The SQLPS module loads and registers SQL Server snap-ins and related assemblies.

Starting from SQL Server 2012, when you launch the mini-shell from SSMS, it loads a full PowerShell console and loads the SQLPS module by default. Instead of going through the mini-shell, you can also alternatively pull up a regular PowerShell console (or ISE) and import the SQLPS module using the `Import-Module` cmdlet introduced in PowerShell v2:

```
Administrator: Windows PowerShell ISE                        _ □ X
File  Edit  View  Tools  Debug  Add-ons  Help

Untitled8.ps1*(Recovered) X

   1    Import-Module SQLPS


PS C:\Windows\system32> Import-Module SQLPS
WARNING: The names of some imported commands from the module 'SQLPS' include una
pproved verbs that might make them less discoverable. To find the commands with
unapproved verbs, run the Import-Module command again with the Verbose parameter
. For a list of approved verbs, type Get-Verb.

PS SQLSERVER:\>
```

Before importing SQLPS, you should set the Execution Policy setting to at least RemoteSigned (or the less restrictive, Unrestricted), otherwise you will encounter errors.

When you import SQLPS, you will notice a warning message appear about unapproved verbs. This is because some cmdlets in this module have *unapproved* names; that is, some verbs used in the cmdlets are not listed in the official verbs that Microsoft endorses in the Get-Verb cmdlet. The specific cmdlets that violate these rules are Encode-Sqlname and Decode-Sqlname.

To avoid seeing these unapproved verb errors, you can use the DisableNameChecking switch:

```
Import-Module SQLPS -DisableNameChecking
```

PowerShell modules also support the autoloading of modules. This feature allows a module to be imported automatically if any cmdlets or functions are used, even without explicitly importing the module. The only requirement is that this module needs to be in a directory listed in the $PSModulePath environment variable (notice $PSModulePath is an environment variable, not a special PowerShell variable unlike $PSVersionTable). The SQLPS module path is added to this variable by default:

Once the SQLPS module is imported, you will see that the `SqlServer` provider has been loaded as a `PSProvider` option in your session:

The same is true for `PSDrive`. Once the module is imported, you will be able to see a new `SQLSERVER` type, `PSDrive`, in your session:

SQL Server snap-ins

PowerShell snap-ins, as introduced in *Chapter 1, Getting Started with PowerShell*, are binaries or **dynamic linked libraries (DLLs)** that were compiled from .NET code. They contain additional cmdlets, functionalities, and even PowerShell providers.

There were two snap-ins provided for SQL Server specifically in SQL Server 2008: `SqlServerCmdletSnapin100` and `SqlServerProviderSnapin100`. Note that the number "100" stands for SQL Server 2008 (or version 10.0). There aren't any other version-specific snap-ins made available for other SQL Server versions.

If you are still working with SQL Server 2008 or SQL Server 2008 R2, you will need to add these snap-ins within the full PowerShell console to use SQL Server-specific cmdlets. You cannot add these snap-ins using the mini-shell (or `sqlps`) utility that comes with SQL Server 2008/R2 because of the built-in constraints in the mini-shell.

To check whether snap-ins have already been loaded, you can use the following commands:

```
Get-PSSnapin SqlServerCmdletSnapin100
Get-PSSnapin SqlServerProviderSnapin100
```

If they are not loaded yet, you can add them using the Add-PSSnapin cmdlet:

```
Add-PSSnapin SqlServerCmdletSnapin100
Add-PSSnapin SqlServerProviderSnapin100
```

Remember that if you are working with SQL Server 2012 onwards and PowerShell V2 and later, you do not need to add these snap-ins. You can just load the SQLPS module in a full PowerShell console, which loads the same SQL Server-related functionalities into your shell.

SQL Server assemblies

Yet another way to work with SQL Server is by loading SQL Server-related assemblies directly. If you were working with SQL Server 2005 and PowerShell V1, when neither the `sqlps` utility nor module were available, this may be the only way to work with PowerShell and SQL Server.

Loading assemblies, however, is not limited to SQL Server-related DLLs. Regardless of the SQL Server version you're working with, you may still want to load other .NET assemblies and use them in your PowerShell session. For example, you may want to load `System.Windows.Forms` if you are utilizing any Windows form components in your PowerShell script.

You can use the same method if you want to load any other .NET assemblies and make use of them in your PowerShell session.

In PowerShell v1, the popular way to load assemblies is by using the `LoadWithPartialName()` method from the `Reflection.Assembly` class. It loads the specified assembly from the application directory or the **Global Assembly Cache (GAC)**.

To load the assemblies, you can use the following command:

```
[void] [Reflection.Assembly] ::LoadWithPartialName
  ("Microsoft.SqlServer.Smo")
```

> Note that `LoadWithPartialName()` is obsolete as of .NET 3.5. `LoadWithPartialName()` is only being shown here in case you need to use it in an older system or if you see it in older books or documentation.

Another, and still valid, way of loading assemblies is by using the `Load()` method from the same `Reflection.Assembly` class. This is an overloaded method, meaning you can provide different sets of parameters for the same method, as long as the parameter signatures are valid and match exactly one overloaded method definition.

Here is an example of loading an assembly called `Microsoft.SqlServer.Smo` for SQL Server 2005. Note the assembly's fully qualified name has been provided to the method:

```
[void] [Reflection.Assembly] ::Load("Microsoft.SqlServer.Smo,
Version=9.0.242.0,
  Culture=neutral, PublicKeyToken=89845dcd8080cc91")
```

If you are using PowerShell v2 and later, you can use the `Add-Type` cmdlet instead of using the `Load()` method:

```
Add-Type -AssemblyName "Microsoft.SqlServer.Smo"
```

Note that starting from SQL Server 2012, you can simply import the SQLPS module, and it will load these assemblies in your PowerShell session.

SQL Server-specific cmdlets

To get the cmdlets and functions that come with SQL Server-related modules, you can use the following command:

```
Get-Command -Module *SQL*
```

The following table lists the cmdlets included in the SQLPS module in a typical SQL Server 2014 installation. You can use this as a reference when you are looking up SQL Server cmdlets. You will notice that there are two SQL Server modules: SQLPS and SQLASCMDLETS. SQLPS contains mostly database engine cmdlets, while the SQLASCMDLETS module contains cmdlets related to SQL Server Analysis Services.

Module name	Command type	Name
SQLPS	Function	SQLSERVER:
SQLASCMDLETS	Cmdlet	Add-RoleMember
SQLPS	Cmdlet	Add-SqlAvailabilityDatabase
SQLPS	Cmdlet	Add-SqlAvailabilityGroupListenerStaticIp
SQLPS	Cmdlet	Add-SqlFirewallRule
SQLASCMDLETS	Cmdlet	Backup-ASDatabase
SQLPS	Cmdlet	Backup-SqlDatabase
SQLPS	Cmdlet	Convert-UrnToPath
SQLPS	Cmdlet	Decode-SqlName
SQLPS	Cmdlet	Disable-SqlAlwaysOn
SQLPS	Cmdlet	Enable-SqlAlwaysOn
SQLPS	Cmdlet	Encode-SqlName
SQLPS	Cmdlet	Get-SqlCredential
SQLPS	Cmdlet	Get-SqlDatabase
SQLPS	Cmdlet	Get-SqlInstance
SQLPS	Cmdlet	Get-SqlSmartAdmin
SQLASCMDLETS	Cmdlet	Invoke-ASCmd
SQLPS	Cmdlet	Invoke-PolicyEvaluation
SQLASCMDLETS	Cmdlet	Invoke-ProcessCube
SQLASCMDLETS	Cmdlet	Invoke-ProcessDimension
SQLASCMDLETS	Cmdlet	Invoke-ProcessPartition
SQLPS	Cmdlet	Invoke-Sqlcmd
SQLPS	Cmdlet	Join-SqlAvailabilityGroup
SQLASCMDLETS	Cmdlet	Merge-Partition
SQLASCMDLETS	Cmdlet	New-RestoreFolder
SQLASCMDLETS	Cmdlet	New-RestoreLocation
SQLPS	Cmdlet	New-SqlAvailabilityGroup
SQLPS	Cmdlet	New-SqlAvailabilityGroupListener
SQLPS	Cmdlet	New-SqlAvailabilityReplica

Module name	Command type	Name
SQLPS	Cmdlet	New-SqlBackupEncryptionOption
SQLPS	Cmdlet	New-SqlCredential
SQLPS	Cmdlet	New-SqlHADREndpoint
SQLASCMDLETS	Cmdlet	Remove-RoleMember
SQLPS	Cmdlet	Remove-SqlAvailabilityDatabase
SQLPS	Cmdlet	Remove-SqlAvailabilityGroup
SQLPS	Cmdlet	Remove-SqlAvailabilityReplica
SQLPS	Cmdlet	Remove-SqlCredential
SQLPS	Cmdlet	Remove-SqlFirewallRule
SQLASCMDLETS	Cmdlet	Restore-ASDatabase
SQLPS	Cmdlet	Restore-SqlDatabase
SQLPS	Cmdlet	Resume-SqlAvailabilityDatabase
SQLPS	Cmdlet	Set-SqlAuthenticationMode
SQLPS	Cmdlet	Set-SqlAvailabilityGroup
SQLPS	Cmdlet	Set-SqlAvailabilityGroupListener
SQLPS	Cmdlet	Set-SqlAvailabilityReplica
SQLPS	Cmdlet	Set-SqlCredential
SQLPS	Cmdlet	Set-SqlHADREndpoint
SQLPS	Cmdlet	Set-SqlNetworkConfiguration
SQLPS	Cmdlet	Set-SqlSmartAdmin
SQLPS	Cmdlet	Start-SqlInstance
SQLPS	Cmdlet	Stop-SqlInstance
SQLPS	Cmdlet	Suspend-SqlAvailabilityDatabase
SQLPS	Cmdlet	Switch-SqlAvailabilityGroup
SQLPS	Cmdlet	Test-SqlAvailabilityGroup
SQLPS	Cmdlet	Test-SqlAvailabilityReplica
SQLPS	Cmdlet	Test-SqlDatabaseReplicaState
SQLPS	Cmdlet	Test-SqlSmartAdmin

SQL Server Management Objects

The SQLPS module exposes over 50 SQL Server-related cmdlets as of SQL Server 2014. This may seem more than a handful, but these cmdlets only cover a fraction of what you may want to do with SQL Server. There will be times when you may want to programmatically manage SQL Server, and SMO may be the most flexible way to do this.

SMO allows you to have programmatic access to SQL Server objects using languages such as VB.NET, C#, and PowerShell.

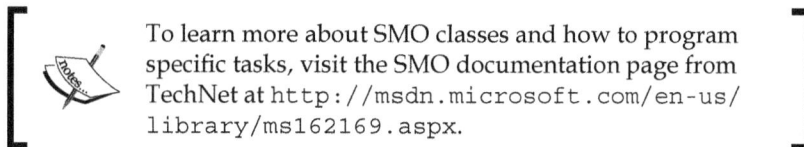

> To learn more about SMO classes and how to program specific tasks, visit the SMO documentation page from TechNet at http://msdn.microsoft.com/en-us/library/ms162169.aspx.

To install SMO, you need to run the SQL Server setup binary and select **Client Tools SDK** in the **Features Selection** window:

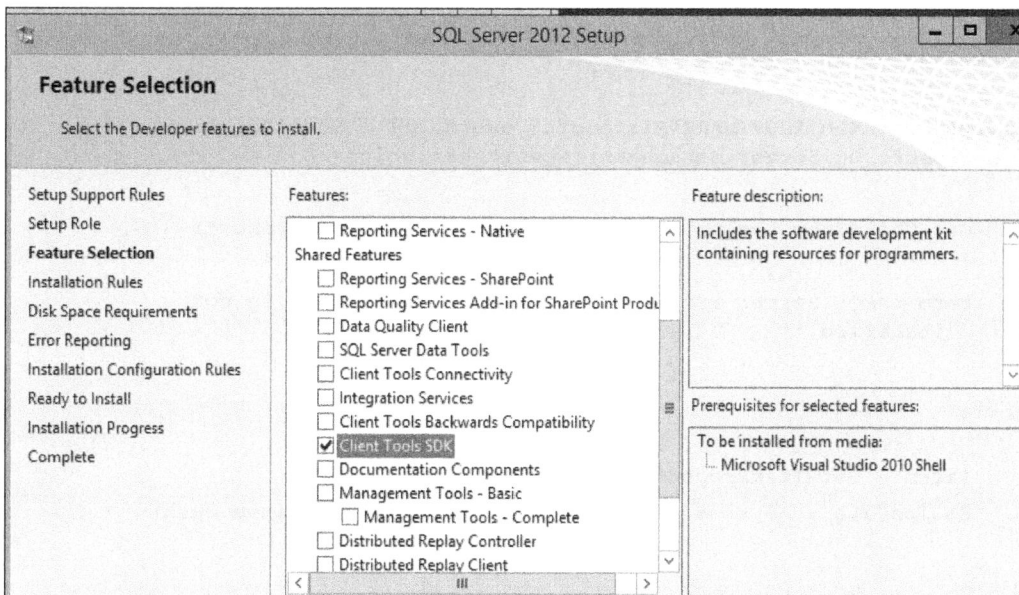

Once installed, the SMO namespaces that become available with SQL Server 2014 are as follows:

* `Microsoft.SqlServer.Management.Smo`
* `Microsoft.SqlServer.Management.Common`

- `Microsoft.SqlServer.Management.Smo.Agent`
- `Microsoft.SqlServer.Management.Smo.Wmi`
- `Microsoft.SqlServer.Management.Smo.RegisteredServers`
- `Microsoft.SqlServer.Management.Smo.Mail`
- `Microsoft.SqlServer.Management.Smo.Broker`

SMO is also available as a separate download. You can search Microsoft Download Center for version-specific packages. Use the term, **Microsoft SQL Server Feature Pack**. The package for SQL Server 2014 can be downloaded from `http://www.microsoft.com/en-us/download/details.aspx?id=42295`.

If you are using SMO assemblies in scripts that do not use the SQL Server PowerShell provider, this is how you can load the SMO assemblies, as documented in the TechNet (`http://msdn.microsoft.com/en-us/library/hh245202.aspx`):

```
#
# Loads the SQL Server Management Objects (SMO)
#

$ErrorActionPreference = "Stop"

$sqlpsreg="HKLM:\SOFTWARE\Microsoft\PowerShell\1\ShellIds\
  Microsoft.SqlServer.Management.PowerShell.sqlps"

if (Get-ChildItem $sqlpsreg -ErrorAction "SilentlyContinue")
{
    throw "SQL Server Provider for Windows PowerShell is not
      installed."
}
else
{
    $item = Get-ItemProperty $sqlpsreg
    $sqlpsPath = [System.IO.Path]::GetDirectoryName($item.Path)
}

$assemblylist =
"Microsoft.SqlServer.Management.Common",
"Microsoft.SqlServer.Smo",
"Microsoft.SqlServer.Dmf ",
"Microsoft.SqlServer.Instapi ",
"Microsoft.SqlServer.SqlWmiManagement ",
```

```
"Microsoft.SqlServer.ConnectionInfo ",
"Microsoft.SqlServer.SmoExtended ",
"Microsoft.SqlServer.SqlTDiagM ",
"Microsoft.SqlServer.SString ",
"Microsoft.SqlServer.Management.RegisteredServers ",
"Microsoft.SqlServer.Management.Sdk.Sfc ",
"Microsoft.SqlServer.SqlEnum ",
"Microsoft.SqlServer.RegSvrEnum ",
"Microsoft.SqlServer.WmiEnum ",
"Microsoft.SqlServer.ServiceBrokerEnum ",
"Microsoft.SqlServer.ConnectionInfoExtended ",
"Microsoft.SqlServer.Management.Collector ",
"Microsoft.SqlServer.Management.CollectorEnum",
"Microsoft.SqlServer.Management.Dac",
"Microsoft.SqlServer.Management.DacEnum",
"Microsoft.SqlServer.Management.Utility"

foreach ($asm in $assemblylist)
{
    $asm = [Reflection.Assembly]::LoadWithPartialName($asm)
}

Push-Location
cd $sqlpsPath
update-FormatData -prependpath SQLProvider.Format.ps1xml
Pop-Location
```

Note that for SQL Server 2012 and later, you do not need to load SMO assemblies explicitly. Importing the SQLPS module loads these assemblies for you. With PowerShell V3 onwards, since these versions support the autoloading of a module, you also don't have to explicitly import SQLPS (although it's strongly recommended you do this). Simply using cmdlets or functions inside the module will autoload the SQLPS module.

Creating SMO objects

To use SMO effectively, you need to know how to create and access SQL Server objects you need and how to explore the methods and properties that are available with each one.

When working with SMO, you will need to create and instantiate SQL Server objects. The following is a simple example:

```
Import-Module SQLPS -DisableNameChecking


#default SQL Server 2014 instance, ie servername
#if the default instance is in your local machine,
#you can simply type "localhost"


$instance = "ROGUE" #or localhost


#instantiate an SMO server object
$server = New-Object `
        -TypeName Microsoft.SqlServer.Management.Smo.Server `
        -ArgumentList $instance


#list some server properties
$server |
Select Name, Version, Status, `
        ConnectionContext, ComputerNamePhysicalNetBIOS
```

Your result will look similar to the following screenshot:

```
Name                        : ROGUE
Version                     : 12.0.2000
Status                      : Online
ConnectionContext           : Data Source=ROGUE;Integrated Security=True;Multip
                              leActiveResultSets=False;Application Name="SQL
                              Management"
ComputerNamePhysicalNetBIOS : ROGUE
```

Let's walk through the script. PowerShell scripts that work with SQL Server usually start with a line that imports the SQLPS module:

```
Import-Module SQLPS -DisableNameChecking
```

Once loaded, you will often need to create an SMO server object. For many tasks, you will need a server object, which can be created as shown in the following snippet:

```
$server   = New-Object `
            -TypeName Microsoft.SqlServer.Management.Smo.Server `
            -ArgumentList $instance
```

To create the object, you need to use the `Microsoft.SqlServer.Management.Smo.Server` class and provide it with a server instance name. Remember that backticks are line continuation characters only. They are included here for readability, but you can also opt to put this code into a single, non-breaking line if you prefer.

Once created, the server object allows you to browse properties, methods, and other objects that belong to the server. You can pipe the server object to a `Select-Object` cmdlet (or simply use `Select` if you want to use the shortened version) to view only a few properties and methods:

```
#list some properties
$server |
Select-Object Name, Version, Status, ConnectionContext, `
    ComputerNamePhysicalNetBIOS
```

Alternatively, you can use the `Get-Member` cmdlet to see the complete list of related properties, methods, functions, and objects:

```
$server | Get-Member
```

Technet provides an SMO Object Model Diagram (available at `http://msdn.microsoft.com/en-us/library/ms162209.aspx`) that can guide you through the object hierarchy:

The preceding screenshot should give you an idea of how expansive the SMO class hierarchy is. This also suggests that we can programmatically access and manage many SQL Server objects. This is good because this means we can accomplish many tasks through scripting with PowerShell.

Summary

In this chapter, we covered different ways to work with PowerShell with SQL Server using PowerShell. The approach you will take will depend on the version of SQL Server and PowerShell that is available in your environment. Loading the SQLPS module is the current de facto way to go to load SQL Server-specific modules and providers. If you need more programmatic access and flexibility, SMO can take you a long way.

In the next chapter, we will cover how to profile and configure SQL Server using PowerShell.

3
Profiling and Configuring SQL Server

When working with SQL Server, usually one of the first tasks is to profile the current instance(s) and environment. This chapter will cover how to quickly profile SQL Server and identify services, instances, settings, and current resources and configurations. This chapter will also introduce you to using **Windows Management Instrumentation (WMI)** and SQL Server SMO classes to profile and configure SQL Server.

The snippets in this chapter will require the full PowerShell console, run with administrative privileges. Some of the topics we'll cover include how to:

- Check server resources (such as CPU, memory, disk space, and network)
- Check hotfixes and service packs
- Check current SQL Server instances
- Check services and service accounts
- Check SQL Server logs
- List current instance configurations
- Change configurations
- Start or stop services
- Change service accounts
- Change instance settings

Current server resources

One of the first things you might want to check out before profiling SQL Server instances is the general health of the server. There are a number of metrics you can check, but usually there are four that you almost always need to check first: processor usage, available disks and their usage, available memory and its usage, and the network.

The **Task Manager** option in Windows can often provide a good at-a-glance view of resources. One way to launch this tool is by right-clicking on the task bar and selecting **Task Manager**, as shown in the following screenshot:

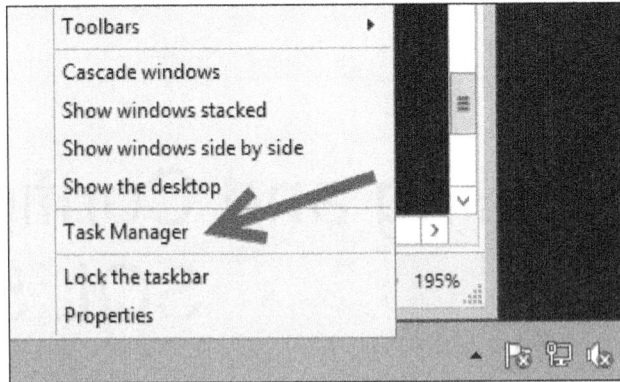

When the **Task Manager** window comes up, you can select the **Processes** tab to see the CPU and memory usage right away. The following screenshot shows what **Task Manager** looks like in Windows Server 2012 R2. This window will look slightly different if you are using a different Windows version:

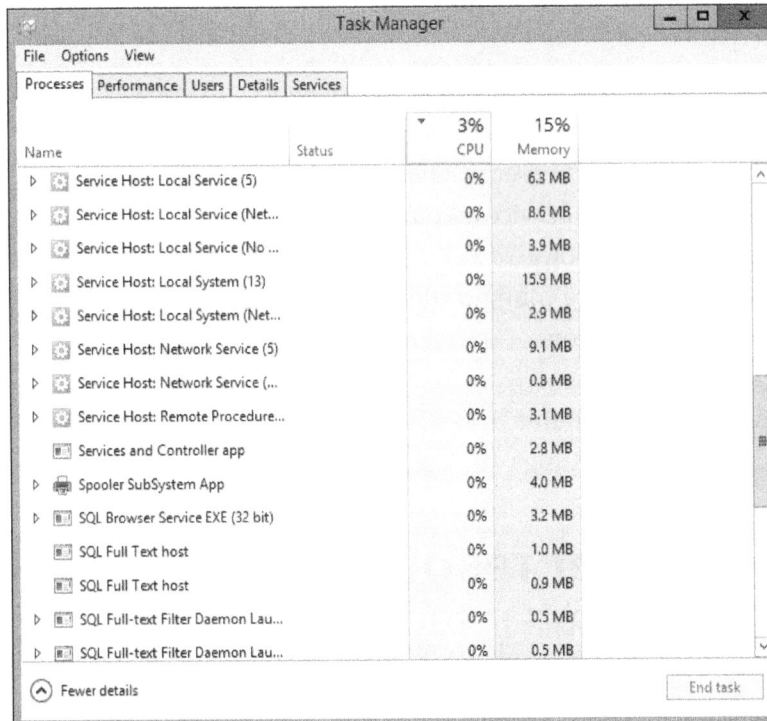

This window can provide a very quick way to figure out which processes are taking up the most CPU or memory. You can click on the **CPU** or **Memory** option to sort data according to those metrics.

Getting processor (CPU) information

The number of processors in a server and their usage can indicate whether SQL Server can perform well on a current server. It is also important to know this when you tune SQL Server later for parallelism.

We can take advantage of the WMI cmdlets and classes available in PowerShell while querying CPU information.

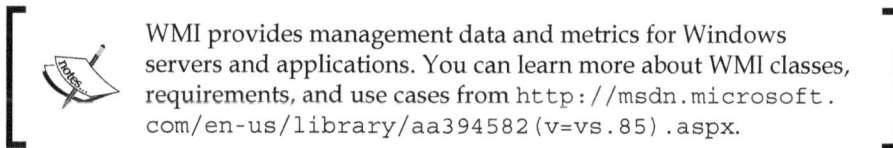

> WMI provides management data and metrics for Windows servers and applications. You can learn more about WMI classes, requirements, and use cases from http://msdn.microsoft.com/en-us/library/aa394582(v=vs.85).aspx.

First, let's identify how many physical processors and cores there are in the server. We can do this by using the Get-WmiObject cmdlet with the Win32_ComputerSystem WMI class:

```
#current server name
#this can be the machine name (in my case ROGUE)
#or simply localhost, if the default instance is installed
$servername = "ROGUE" #or localhost


Get-WmiObject -Class Win32_ComputerSystem `
              -ComputerName $servername |
Select-Object Name,
      Domain,
      NumberOfProcessors,
      NumberOfLogicalProcessors |
Format-List
```

The preceding script displays the current server name and domain. In addition, the NumberOfProcessors property indicates the physical processors detected, and NumberOfLogicalProcessors indicates the number of cores. Your result will look like the following screenshot:

```
Name                        :  ROGUE
Domain                      :  queryworks.local
NumberOfProcessors          :  2
NumberOfLogicalProcessors   :  4
```

To query the CPU usage, we can use the Win32_Processor WMI class. This class exposes the LoadPercentage property for each processor, which can be aggregated to get an average value.

> Please visit http://msdn.microsoft.com/en-us/ library/aa394373(v=vs.85).aspx to learn more about the syntax, properties, and enumeration values available with the Win32_processor WMI class.

The following is the snippet that gets you the current CPU usage:

```
#current server name
$servername = "ROGUE"


Get-WmiObject -Class Win32_Processor -ComputerName $servername |
Measure-Object -Property LoadPercentage –Average
```

A sample result looks like the following screenshot:

```
Count    :  2
Average  :  3
Sum      :
Maximum  :
Minimum  :
Property :  LoadPercentage
```

We piped the result of the Get-WmiObject cmdlet to the Measure-Object cmdlet. The Measure-Object cmdlet allows you to generate quick statistics in PowerShell. In the preceding snippet, we got the average LoadPercentage value from two physical processors.

The `Measure-Object` cmdlet is useful when you are measuring `LoadPercentage` from multiple physical processors because each one will have its own `LoadPercentage` value. If you have a single processor, you can simply use the following:

```
$(Get-WmiObject -Class Win32_Processor -
  ComputerName $servername).LoadPercentage
```

Checking server memory

In addition to CPU usage, we also want to see how much physical memory is available on the server that SQL Server is sitting on and how much memory is being used. Using the `Get-WmiObject` cmdlet and this time with the `Win32_OperatingSystem` class, we can check this information using PowerShell.

First, let's check what *types* of memory we can query from this class. Note that you need to run the following sample in a full PowerShell console. The following snippet also uses a new `Where-Object` syntax, available only with PowerShell v3 and later:

```
Get-WmiObject -Class Win32_OperatingSystem `
              -ComputerName $servername |
Get-Member -MemberType Property |
Where-Object Name -Like "*Mem*" |
Select-Object Name
```

You will get a few properties in the `Win32_OperatingSystem` WMI class related to memory:

```
Name
----
FreePhysicalMemory
FreeVirtualMemory
MaxProcessMemorySize
TotalVirtualMemorySize
TotalVisibleMemorySize
```

Note that there are other WMI classes that can get you additional memory metrics and properties, such as `Win32_PhysicalMemory` and `Win32_MemoryDevice`. For our script, let's use `Win32_OperatingSystem` WMI class's properties, namely `TotalVisibleMemorySize` and `FreePhysicalMemory`, and calculate `MemoryUsage`.

`TotalVisibleMemorySize` provides the total physical memory in KB installed and accessible to the operating system. `FreePhysicalMemory` is the current free memory available in KB. From these two metrics, we can calculate the memory usage:

```
MemoryUsage = ((TotalVisibleMemorySize - FreePhysicalMemory) * 100)/
    TotalVisibleMemorySize
```

The following is the PowerShell snippet that returns the aforementioned three values:

```
Get-WmiObject -Class Win32_OperatingSystem -
  ComputerName $servername |
Select-Object @{Name="TotalVisibleMemorySize (GB)";
  Expression={"{0:N1}" -f (($_.TotalVisibleMemorySize)/1024/1024)}},
@{Name="FreePhysicalMemory (GB)";Expression={"{0:N1}" -
  f (($_.FreePhysicalMemory)/1024/1024)}},
@{Name="MemoryUsage %";Expression={ "{0:N2}" -
  f ((($_.TotalVisibleMemorySize - $_.FreePhysicalMemory)*100)
  / $_.TotalVisibleMemorySize) }} |
Format-List
```

Don't worry if the preceding snippet looks a little bit confusing. We will walk through parts of the code. The snippet uses an advanced PowerShell construct called calculated properties, which is used with `Select-Object` and allows you to create (that is, calculate) a property that an object may not inherently have.

Let's look at one part of the code:

```
Select-Object @{Name="TotalVisibleMemorySize (GB)";
  Expression={"{0:N1}" -f (($_.TotalVisibleMemorySize)/1024/1024)}}
```

Right besides `Select-Object` is an expression that looks like the following:

```
@{Name="Name";Expression={"Expression" -f format}}
```

This is the calculated property. It has a name-value pair, enclosed in `@{}`. The value you provide in `Name` will be the new property name, and the value (or expression) in the `Expression` field will be the new property value.

> To learn more about PowerShell's calculated properties and check out additional examples, you can visit http://technet.microsoft.com/en-us/library/ff730948.aspx.

Thus, in our code, we create three new properties (with formatted values) that the `Win32_OperatingSystem` class does not inherently have: `TotalVisibleMemorySize` `(GB)`, `FreePhysicalMemory` `(GB)`, and `MemoryUsage` `%`. To make `TotalVisibleMemorySize` `(GB)` and `FreePhysicalMemory` `(GB)` more readable, the values were in **Gigabyte (GB)** units, for example:

```
Expression={"{0:N1}" -f (($_.TotalVisibleMemorySize)/1024/1024)}}
```

The result that you get will look like the following screenshot:

```
TotalVisibleMemorySize (GB) : 10.7
FreePhysicalMemory (GB)     : 9.1
MemoryUsage %               : 15.43
```

The `-f` operator is a string formatting operator. What we've done is created a placeholder `"{0:N1}"` and indicated a replacement value, which is the expression that follows `-f`. There is a good reference available at `http://blogs.technet.com/b/heyscriptingguy/archive/2013/03/11/understanding-powershell-and-basic-string-formatting.aspx` that talks about different ways of formatting strings in PowerShell.

Checking disk space

To figure out the available disk drives and disk space in your server, you can use the `Win32_LogicalDisk` WMI class. We can list the `DeviceID`, `DriveType`, `Size`, and `FreeSpace`. From `Size` and `FreeSpace`, we can calculate the percentage of disk space that's still free.

The snippet to get the disk information is presented as follows:

```
#current server name
$servername = "ROGUE"


Get-WmiObject -Class Win32_LogicalDisk `
      -ComputerName $servername |
Select-Object @{Name="DeviceID";Expression={$_.DeviceID}},
      @{Name="DriveType";
        Expression={switch ($_.DriveType)
              {
                  0 {"Unknown"}
                  1 {"No Root Directory"}
                  2 {"Removable Disk"}
```

```
                    3 {"Local Disk"}
                    4 {"Network Drive"}
                    5 {"Compact Disc"}
                    6 {"RAM Disk"}
                }};
    },
    @{Name="Size (GB)";Expression={"{0:N1}" -f($_.Size/1GB)}},
    @{Name="Free Space (GB)";Expression={"{0:N1}" -
      f($_.FreeSpace/1GB)}},
    @{Name="Free Space (%)";
      Expression={
        if ($_.Size -gt 0)
        {
            "{0:P0}" -f($_.FreeSpace/$_.Size)
        }
        else
        {
            0
        }
      }
    } |
Format-Table -AutoSize
```

In the code, we replaced the DriveType value with a more readable description, as described in MSDN (available at http://msdn.microsoft.com/en-us/library/ aa394173(v=vs.85).aspx). We also represented the Size and FreeSpace values in GB. When calculating the percentage of free space, we want to avoid a division-by-zero error. This is why we first checked whether the size was greater than zero (0).

The result should look as shown in the following screenshot:

```
DeviceID DriveType       Size (GB) Free Space (GB) Free Space (%)
-------- ---------       --------- --------------- --------------
A:       Removable Disk  0.0       0.0                          0
C:       Local Disk      120.0     99.9                      83 %
D:       Compact Disc    3.6       0.0                        0 %
```

In the preceding example, we simply listed all the drives in the system. You can narrow the script down to only look at local or non-removable disks by adding a filter to your Get-WmiObject invocation:

```
Get-WmiObject -Class Win32_LogicalDisk –Filter "DriveType=3" `
    -ComputerName $servername
```

Checking network settings

To get the network interfaces in your server, you can use the Win32_NetworkAdapter Configuration WMI class. There are a number of properties that can be queried, including the network card description, IP address, and MAC address:

```
Get-WmiObject -Class Win32_NetworkAdapterConfiguration `
        -ComputerName $servername `
        -Filter IPEnabled=True |
Select-Object Description, DHCPEnabled,
        IPEnabled, IPAddress,
        MACAddress
```

This script will list out all IP-enabled network interfaces because we added the filter IPEnabled=True and display a number of fields, including the IP and MAC address values:

```
Description : Intel(R) 82574L Gigabit Network Connection
DHCPEnabled : True
IPEnabled   : True
IPAddress   : {192.168.111.129, fe80::6df1:881d:72f5:edb}
MACAddress  : 00:0C:29:DF:F0:41

Description : Intel(R) 82574L Gigabit Network Connection #2
DHCPEnabled : False
IPEnabled   : True
IPAddress   : {10.0.0.20, fe80::7052:5a0:8c8c:5753}
MACAddress  : 00:0C:29:DF:F0:4B
```

Hotfixes and service packs

We can use PowerShell to figure out the operating system the server is running on and on which service pack. The Win32_OperatingSystem WMI class contains the OS service pack information. The following script performs this query:

```
#current server name
$servername = "ROGUE"


Get-WmiObject -Class Win32_OperatingSystem `
            -ComputerName $servername |
Select-Object CSName, Caption,
        ServicePackMajorVersion,
        ServicePackMinorVersion |
Format-List
```

Your result should include the computer name and the service pack information. If you get a zero (0) value, it means no service packs have been applied to the system yet.

```
CSName                      : ROGUE
Caption                     : Microsoft Windows Server 2012 R2 Standard
ServicePackMajorVersion : 0
ServicePackMinorVersion : 0
```

In addition to service pack information, you can also use PowerShell to query which hotfixes and updates have been installed on the system. You can use the `Win32_QuickFixEngineering` WMI class to do this. The following is an example of how you can use this class:

```
#current server name
$servername = "ROGUE"


Get-WmiObject -Class Win32_QuickFixEngineering `
            -ComputerName $servername |
Sort-Object -Property InstalledOn -Descending |
Format-Table -AutoSize
```

Your result will look similar to the following screenshot:

```
Source Description       HotFixID  InstalledBy        InstalledOn
------ -----------       --------  -----------        -----------
ROGUE  Update            KB2995004 NT AUTHORITY\SYSTEM 10/3/2014 12:00:00 AM
ROGUE  Update            KB2990532 NT AUTHORITY\SYSTEM 10/3/2014 12:00:00 AM
ROGUE  Update            KB2979582 NT AUTHORITY\SYSTEM 10/3/2014 12:00:00 AM
ROGUE  Update            KB2975719 NT AUTHORITY\SYSTEM 10/3/2014 12:00:00 AM
ROGUE  Update            KB2993100 NT AUTHORITY\SYSTEM 9/18/2014 12:00:00 AM
ROGUE  Security Update   KB2988948 NT AUTHORITY\SYSTEM 9/13/2014 12:00:00 AM
ROGUE  Security Update   KB2977765 NT AUTHORITY\SYSTEM 9/13/2014 12:00:00 AM
ROGUE  Security Update   KB2977629 NT AUTHORITY\SYSTEM 9/13/2014 12:00:00 AM
ROGUE  Security Update   KB2973114 NT AUTHORITY\SYSTEM 9/13/2014 12:00:00 AM
ROGUE  Security Update   KB2972213 NT AUTHORITY\SYSTEM 9/13/2014 12:00:00 AM
```

The results will most likely exceed the scrollable limit of your PowerShell window, so you may want to pipe the results to a file to get the complete list. Be careful, however. `Win32_QuickFixEngineering` does not report all updates and hotfixes. According to MSDN, updates via **Microsoft Installer** (**MSI**) or the Windows Update site are not reported by this class.

This is the definition of the class in MSDN (available at `http://msdn.microsoft.com/en-us/library/aa394391(v=vs.85).aspx`):

> *"The* `Win32_QuickFixEngineering` *WMI class represents a small system-wide update, commonly referred to as a quick-fix engineering (QFE) update, applied to the current operating system. Starting with Windows Vista, this class returns only the updates supplied by Component Based Servicing (CBS). These updates are not listed in the registry. Updates supplied by Microsoft Windows Installer (MSI) or the Windows update site (*`http://update.microsoft.com`*) are not returned by* `Win32_QuickFixEngineering`*."*

Current SQL Server instances

You should also check how many SQL Server instances are installed on the server and their names for non-default instances. To do this, we can use **SQL Management Objects** (**SMO**) with PowerShell and then use the `ServerInstances` member property:

```
#below should be a single line of code
$managedComputer = New-Object "Microsoft.SqlServer.Management.
  Smo.Wmi.ManagedComputer" $servername


#list SQL Server instances
$managedComputer.ServerInstances |
Select-Object Name, State, ServerProtocols, Urn |
Format-List
```

The preceding script simply lists the instances installed. Note that `MSSQLSERVER` is the name you'll see for a default instance:

```
Name            : MSSQLSERVER
State           : Existing
ServerProtocols : {Np, Sm, Tcp}
Urn             : ManagedComputer[@Name='ROGUE']/ServerInstance[@Name='MSSQLSERVER']

Name            : SQL2014
State           : Existing
ServerProtocols : {Np, Sm, Tcp}
Urn             : ManagedComputer[@Name='ROGUE']/ServerInstance[@Name='SQL2014']
```

Services and service accounts

Once you have identified the instances, you may want to know the SQL Server-related services for each one of the instances. You can use the same SMO class to query the services related to a SQL Server instance. The `Microsoft.SqlServer.Management.Smo.Wmi.ManagedComputer` class has a property called `Services` that lists the services:

```
Import-Module SQLPS -DisableNameChecking


#current server name
$servername = "ROGUE"


$managedComputer = New-Object "Microsoft.SqlServer.Management.Smo.Wmi.ManagedComputer" $servername


$managedComputer.Services |
Select-Object Name, ServiceAccount, DisplayName |
Format-Table -AutoSize
```

You should see a result similar to the following screenshot:

```
Name                          ServiceAccount                      DisplayName
----                          --------------                      -----------
MsDtsServer120                QUERYWORKS\sqlservice               SQL Server Integration Service
MSSQL$SQL2014                 queryworks\sqlservice               SQL Server (SQL2014)
MSSQLFDLauncher               NT Service\MSSQLFDLauncher          SQL Full-text Filter Daemon La
MSSQLFDLauncher$SQL2014       NT Service\MSSQLFDLauncher$SQL2014  SQL Full-text Filter Daemon La
MSSQLSERVER                   QUERYWORKS\sqlservice               SQL Server (MSSQLSERVER)
MSSQLServerOLAPService        QUERYWORKS\sqlservice               SQL Server Analysis Services (
ReportServer                  QUERYWORKS\sqlservice               SQL Server Reporting Services
SQLAgent$SQL2014              queryworks\sqlservice               SQL Server Agent (SQL2014)
SQLBrowser                    NT AUTHORITY\LOCALSERVICE           SQL Server Browser
SQLSERVERAGENT                QUERYWORKS\sqlservice               SQL Server Agent (MSSQLSERVER)
```

You can see that in my instance, I have many services installed, including SQL Server Agent, SQL Server Integration Services, SQL Server Analysis Services, and SQL Server Reporting Services.

SQL Server error logs

You can view error logs in **SQL Server Management Studio (SSMS)**. To view SQL Server-specific errors, you can open up SSMS and expand the **SQL Server Agent** node. Under the **Error Logs** folder, you can see the most recent error and the most recent archived error:

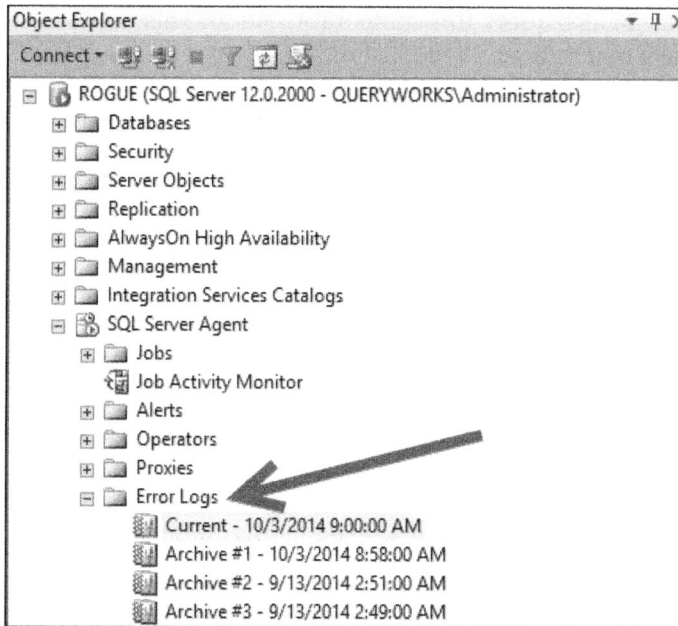

Alternatively, you can go to **Management** and expand **SQL Server Logs**. When you double-click on any one of the error logs, a log file viewer appears. You can select an option to view additional logs from the left-hand side pane. To view the most recent SQL Server-specific logs, check **SQL Server** on the left-hand side pane and then the **Current** checkbox:

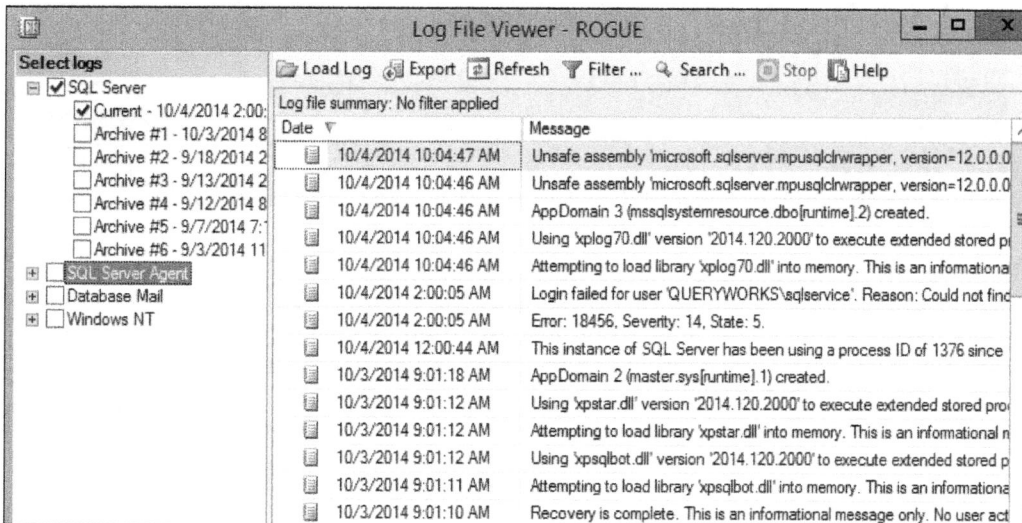

Using SMO, you can also query this same information. This requires creating an SMO server object that references the instance you are working with. Once your server variable is instantiated, you can invoke the `ReadErrorLog()` method. The following snippet shows how you can display the five most recent entries in the SQL Server log:

```
#assuming you already created your SMO server object
$server = New-Object "Microsoft.SqlServer.Management.Smo.Server"
$servername


#display most recent 5 entries
$server.ReadErrorLog() |
Select-Object LogDate, ProcessInfo, Text, HasErrors  -Last 5  |
Format-List
```

The preceding script should give you a result similar to the following screenshot:

```
LogDate      : 10/4/2014 12:00:44 AM
ProcessInfo  : spid29s
Text         : This instance of SQL Server has been using a process ID c
               AM (local) 10/3/2014 4:01:10 PM (UTC). This is an informa
               action is required.
HasErrors    : False

LogDate      : 10/4/2014 2:00:05 AM
ProcessInfo  : Logon
Text         : Error: 18456, Severity: 14, State: 5.
HasErrors    : False

LogDate      : 10/4/2014 2:00:05 AM
ProcessInfo  : Logon
Text         : Login failed for user 'QUERYWORKS\sqlservice'. Reason: Co
               the name provided. [CLIENT: <local machine>]

HasErrors    : False
```

You will have to tweak this script. Most likely, you will want more than just the most recent five entries. You can either change the `-Last` parameter to show more logs or tweak the code and add additional properties and filters based on your needs. For example, if you want to get only the ones that were recorded as errors, then you will have to pipe the result of `$server.ReadErrorLog()` to `Where-Object HasErrors -eq $true` before passing the result to the `Select-Object` cmdlet:

```
$server.ReadErrorLog() |
Where-Object HasErrors -eq $true
```

Current instance configuration

PowerShell makes it easy to query a SQL Server instance and export current configurations. We can make use of the SMO server object and query all the properties. The following is an example script that performs this export:

```
#current server name
$servername = "ROGUE"


$server = New-Object "Microsoft.SqlServer.Management.Smo.
  Server" $servername


$server |
Get-Member |
Where-Object Name -ne "SystemMessages" |
Where-Object MemberType -eq "Property" |
Select-Object Name,
      @{Name="Value";Expression={$server.($_.Name)}} |
Format-Table -AutoSize
```

Once the script runs, you should find all the instance properties and corresponding values displayed on your screen:

```
Name                            Value
----                            -----
ActiveDirectory
AffinityInfo                    Microsoft.SqlServer.Management.Smo.AffinityIn
AuditLevel                      Failure
Audits
AvailabilityGroups
BackupDevices
BackupDirectory                 C:\Program Files\Microsoft SQL Server\MSSQL12
BrowserServiceAccount           NT AUTHORITY\LOCALSERVICE
BrowserStartMode                Auto
BuildClrVersion                 4.0.30319
BuildClrVersionString           v4.0.30319
BuildNumber                     2000
ClusterName
ClusterQuorumState              NotApplicable
ClusterQuorumType               NotApplicable
Collation                       SQL_Latin1_General_CP1_CI_AS
CollationID                     872468488
ComparisonStyle                 196609
ComputerNamePhysicalNetBIOS     ROGUE
Configuration                   Microsoft.SqlServer.Management.Smo.Configurat
ConnectionContext               Data Source=ROGUE;Integrated Security=True;Mu
Credentials
CryptographicProviders
Databases                       {AdventureWorks2014, AdventureWorksLT2012, Ch
DefaultFile                     C:\Program Files\Microsoft SQL Server\MSSQL12
DefaultLog                      C:\Program Files\Microsoft SQL Server\MSSQL12
```

Let's walk through the script. The preceding sample script creates an SMO server object based on the SQL Server instance named ROGUE:

```
#current server name
$servername = "ROGUE" #or localhost


$server = New-Object "Microsoft.SqlServer.Management.Smo.
  Server" $servername
```

Once the SMO server object is created, in our case $server, all the properties of the server are queried except for any system messages:

```
$server |
Get-Member |
Where-Object Name -ne "SystemMessages" |
Where-Object MemberType -eq "Property"
```

The last lines in the block of the preceding snippet display the property name and the value of that property. All of these are displayed in table format in the PowerShell console:

```
Select-Object Name,
     @{Name="Value";Expression={$server.($_.Name)}} |
Format-Table -AutoSize
```

Displaying these properties onscreen is well and good for a visual check. However, if you want to keep track of all these configurations and analyze changes over time, you will need to keep this in a more permanent format. One way to do this is to save the results to a file and safely archive it. To save the results, you simply need to pipe most part of the preceding block, but instead of using Format-Table as the last cmdlet, you can use Export-Csv as the final action:

```
$folder = "C:\Temp"
$currdate = Get-Date -Format "yyyy-MM-dd_hmmtt"


#example filename: ROGUE_2014-10-04_1009AM
$filename = "$($servername)_$($currdate).csv"


$fullpath = Join-Path $folder $filename


$server |
```

```
Get-Member |

Where-Object Name -ne "SystemMessages" |

Where-Object MemberType -eq "Property" |

Select-Object Name,

        @{N="Value";E={$server.($_.Name)}} |

Export-Csv -Path $fullpath -NoTypeInformation
```

The preceding script is simply an example of how to take the configuration results and save it to a CSV file. There are a variety of other options available, such as saving this to an XML or JSON file or even storing it into a SQL Server table.

Changing configurations

PowerShell can help not only audit your current instance configurations, but can also help if you need to manage and change configurations, such as changing service accounts and default backup folders and turning on (or off) some instance- and database-level features.

Start or stop services

There are a handful cmdlets that work with services. To get these cmdlets, you can use the following command:

```
Get-Command -Name "*Service*" -CommandType "Cmdlet"
```

The result you will get is similar to the following screenshot:

```
CommandType        Name
-----------        ----
Cmdlet             Get-Service
Cmdlet             New-Service
Cmdlet             New-WebServiceProxy
Cmdlet             Restart-Service
Cmdlet             Resume-Service
Cmdlet             Set-Service
Cmdlet             Start-Service
Cmdlet             Stop-Service
Cmdlet             Suspend-Service
```

To start or stop services, you can use the `Start-Service` and `Stop-Service` cmdlets. The following snippet is an example of how you can use these cmdlets. In the following example, we are targeting the SQL Server Agent service of a named instance called `SQL2014`. This service can be referred to as `SQLAgent$SQL2014`. Since the $ sign is a special character in PowerShell that signifies variable names, the $ sign in the service name needs to be escaped with a backtick, that is, `"SQLAgent`$SQL2014"`. An alternative is to use single quotes around the named instance's name, which will not require the escape character, that is, `'SQLAgent$SQL2014'`:

```
$servicename = "SQLAgent`$SQL2014"
Stop-Service -Name $servicename
Start-Service -Name $servicename
```

You can start using these service-related cmdlets in any PowerShell scripts you may have that need to go through a list of services and start/stop/restart based on some parameters or conditions.

Changing a service account

Service accounts may need to be updated and changed every now and then. You can see the currently set service accounts if you open up **SQL Server Configuration Manager** and select **SQL Server Services** from the left-hand side pane. The service account can be found in the **Log On As column** option:

Name	State	Start Mode	Log On As	Process ID
SQL Server Integration Services 12.0	Running	Automatic	QUERYWORKS\sqlservice	1272
SQL Server (SQL2014)	Running	Automatic	queryworks\sqlservice	1336
SQL Full-text Filter Daemon Launcher (MSSQLSERVER)	Running	Manual	NT Service\MSSQLFDLauncher	364
SQL Full-text Filter Daemon Launcher (SQL2014)	Running	Manual	NT Service\MSSQLFDLauncher$SQL2014	2344
SQL Server (MSSQLSERVER)	Running	Automatic	QUERYWORKS\sqlservice	1376
SQL Server Analysis Services (MSSQLSERVER)	Running	Automatic	QUERYWORKS\sqlservice	1488
SQL Server Reporting Services (MSSQLSERVER)	Running	Automatic	QUERYWORKS\sqlservice	1528
SQL Server Agent (SQL2014)	Running	Automatic	QUERYWORKS\sqlservice	7784
SQL Server Browser	Running	Automatic	NT AUTHORITY\LOCALSERVICE	1628
SQL Server Agent (MSSQLSERVER)	Running	Automatic	QUERYWORKS\sqlservice	2508

Should you need to change the service accounts for any SQL Server services, you can use PowerShell to streamline the task so you don't even have to open **SQL Server Configuration Manager**.

You can create a `Microsoft.SqlServer.Management.Smo.Wmi.ManagedComputer` object. To change the service account, you can use the `SetServiceAccount()` method. Instead of passing the service account name and password in clear text, you can use the `Get-Credential` cmdlet. This cmdlet opens a logon dialog box and prompts you for the account and password to use.

Here is an example script that changes the service account for `SQLAgent$SQL2014` from `QUERYWORKS\sqlservice` to `QUERYWORKS\sqlagentservice`:

```
Import-Module SQLPS -DisableNameChecking


#current server name
$servername = "ROGUE"


$managedComputer = New-Object "Microsoft.SqlServer.Management.Smo.
  Wmi.ManagedComputer" $servername


$servicename = "SQLAgent`$SQL2014"


$sqlservice = $managedComputer.Services |
            Where-Object Name -EQ $servicename


#check current service account
$sqlservice.ServiceAccount


#set new service account
$newserviceaccount = "QUERYWORKS\sqlagentservice"
$credential = Get-Credential -Credential $newserviceaccount
$sqlservice.SetServiceAccount($credential.UserName,
  $credential.GetNetworkCredential().Password)


#check new service account
$sqlservice.ServiceAccount
```

Once the script is finished, you can confirm from **SQL Server Configuration Manager** that the service account has indeed been updated. You might need to refresh the **SQL Server Configuration Manager** view if you had it opened already before you changed the service account:

Sql Server Configuration Manager				
Name	State	Start Mode	Log On As	Process ID
SQL Server Integration Services 12.0	Running	Automatic	QUERYWORKS\sqlservice	1272
SQL Server (SQL2014)	Running	Automatic	queryworks\sqlservice	1336
SQL Full-text Filter Daemon Launcher (MSSQLSERVER)	Running	Manual	NT Service\MSSQLFDLauncher	364
SQL Full-text Filter Daemon Launcher (SQL2014)	Running	Manual	NT Service\MSSQLFDLauncher$SQL2014	2344
SQL Server (MSSQLSERVER)	Running	Automatic	QUERYWORKS\sqlservice	1376
SQL Server Analysis Services (MSSQLSERVER)	Running	Automatic	QUERYWORKS\sqlservice	1488
SQL Server Reporting Services (MSSQLSERVER)	Running	Automatic	QUERYWORKS\sqlservice	1528
SQL Server Agent (SQL2014)	Running	Automatic	QUERYWORKS\sqlagentservice	1032
SQL Server Browser	Running	Automatic	NT AUTHORITY\LOCALSERVICE	1628
SQL Server Agent (MSSQLSERVER)	Running	Automatic	QUERYWORKS\sqlservice	2508

Changing instance settings

The SMO server class contains many member properties and methods. Some properties are accessible right from the object, but for some, you may need to navigate properties that contain other properties/classes. The best way to explore is by taking the SMO server object and listing down all the members, their methods and properties. You can also use IntelliSense in the PowerShell ISE if you want to explore the properties and methods while you code. All of these properties are also documented in the MSDN link available at `http://msdn.microsoft.com/en-us/library/microsoft.sqlserver.management.smo.server.aspx`.

Many of the properties are updateable. However, there are also a number of properties that are marked as read-only; therefore, they cannot be updated. Just be aware of this.

For the most part, once you've identified an updateable property, you can set the property to the new value and use the `Alter()` method of the server object to make the changes permanent.

The following example shows how you can change the default backup directory of the server. Note that for this example, we will access the `BackupDirectory` member property directly from the `$server` variable:

```
Import-Module SQLPS -DisableNameChecking


#current server name
$servername = "ROGUE"


$server = New-Object "Microsoft.SqlServer.Management.Smo.Server"
$servername


#check current backup directory
$server.BackupDirectory


#change backup directory
$dir = "C:\Temp"
$server.BackupDirectory = $dir
$server.Alter()


#check current backup directory
$server.BackupDirectory
```

Once executed, you can also check the `BackupDirectory` property when you go to
SQL Server Management Studio and right-click on the instance and select **Properties**:

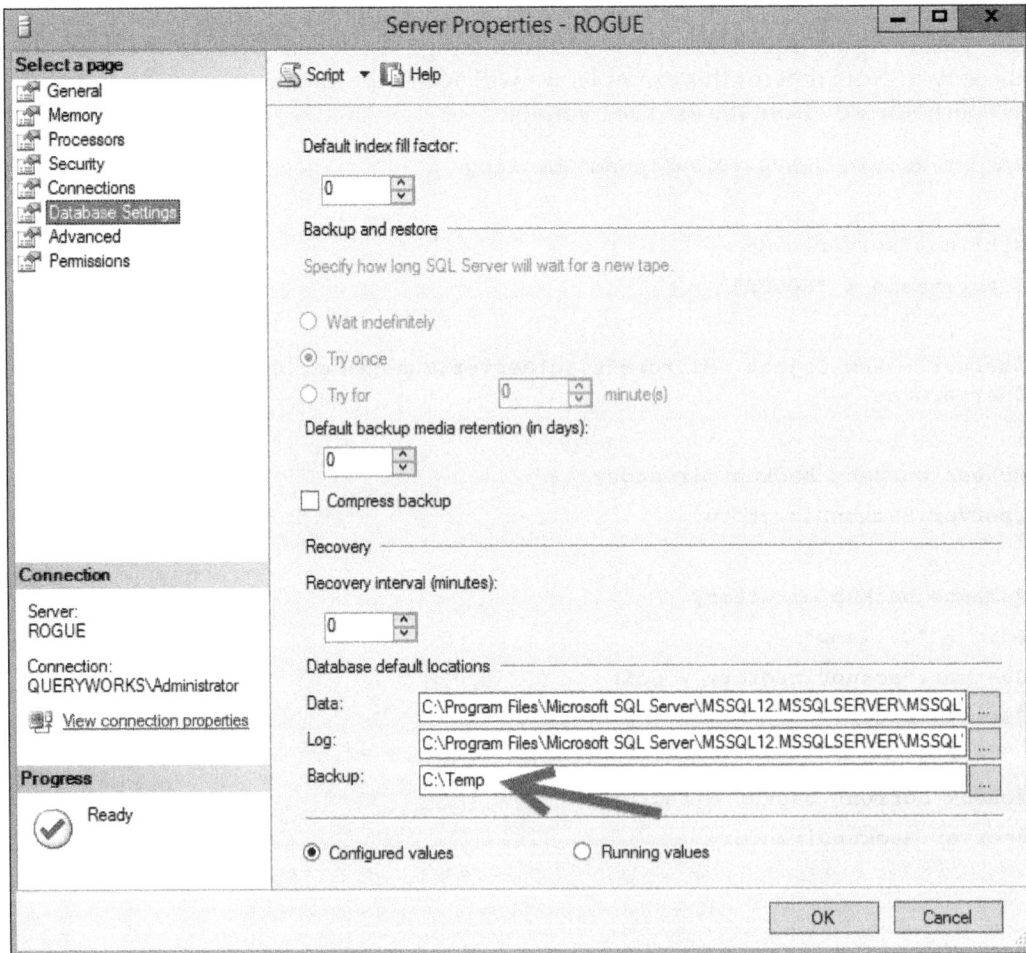

The `Microsoft.SqlServer.Management.Smo.Server` class also has a
`Configuration` property. From this property, you can change settings that you can
normally change using the system-stored procedure, namely `sp_configure`.

The following script shows you how you can enable `xp_cmdshell` using PowerShell:

```
$server.Configuration.XPCmdShellEnabled.ConfigValue = 1

$server.Configuration.Alter()

$server.Configuration.XPCmdShellEnabled
```

Once completed, you should see that for `xp_cmdshell`, `RunValue` will be 1 (meaning it's enabled) and `ConfigValue` will be 1 (meaning it's effective, similar to having run `RECONFIGURE` after `sp_configure`):

```
DisplayName : xp_cmdshell
Number      : 16390
Minimum     : 0
Maximum     : 1
IsDynamic   : True
IsAdvanced  : True
Description : Enable or disable command shell
RunValue    : 1
ConfigValue : 1
```

Note that we are turning the `xp_cmdshell` option on for demonstration purposes only. Since `xp_cmdshell` allows the running of programs and commands from within SQL Server, it is highly recommended that you keep this setting disabled in your system.

For the last example, let's check the settings under the `Settings` property. Once you've created an SMO server object, you can display the properties using the following command:

$server.Settings

The following screenshot shows the values under `Settings`:

```
AuditLevel           : Failure
BackupDirectory      : C:\Program Files\Microsoft SQL Server\MSSQL12.M
DefaultFile          : C:\Program Files\Microsoft SQL Server\MSSQL12.M
DefaultLog           : C:\Program Files\Microsoft SQL Server\MSSQL12.M
LoginMode            : Integrated
MailProfile          :
NumberOfLogFiles     : -1
PerfMonMode          : None
TapeLoadWaitTime     : -1
Parent               : [ROGUE]
OleDbProviderSettings : {ADsDSOObject, MSDAOSP, MSDASQL, MSOLAP...}
Urn                  : Server[@Name='ROGUE']/Setting
Properties           : {Name=AuditLevel/Type=Microsoft.SqlServer.Manag
                       ue/Value=Failure,
                       Name=BackupDirectory/Type=System.String/Writabl
                       Files\Microsoft SQL Server\MSSQL12.MSSQLSERVER\
                       Name=DefaultFile/Type=System.String/Writable=Tr
                       Files\Microsoft SQL Server\MSSQL12.MSSQLSERVER\
                       Name=DefaultLog/Type=System.String/Writable=Tru
                       Files\Microsoft SQL Server\MSSQL12.MSSQLSERVER\
UserData             :
State                : Existing
```

In the next screenshot of the script, we are going to change the `AuditLevel` value of the instance from `Failure` to `All`. This will change the logging behavior of the instance, that is, instead of logging only failed login attempts, both successful and failed login attempts will be recorded.

The property we will change is `Settings.AuditLevel`. This needs to be set to a valid `AuditLevel` enumeration. Normally, this will require that you look up the valid enumeration values from TechNet or MSDN. However, the autocomplete option in PowerShell ISE comes in handy. When you do this in PowerShell ISE, the valid enumeration values will appear once you type in two colons (::) after the class name:

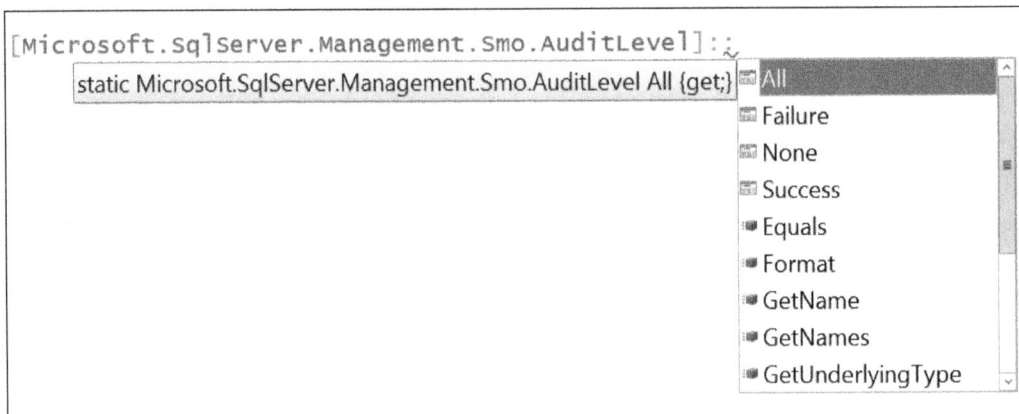

```
[Microsoft.SqlServer.Management.Smo.AuditLevel]::
    static Microsoft.SqlServer.Management.Smo.AuditLevel All {get;}   All
                                                                      Failure
                                                                      None
                                                                      Success
                                                                      Equals
                                                                      Format
                                                                      GetName
                                                                      GetNames
                                                                      GetUnderlyingType
```

The script to change the audit level from `Failure` to `All` looks similar to the following:

```
$server.Settings.AuditLevel = [Microsoft.SqlServer.Management.Smo.
AuditLevel]::All

#make changes permanent
$server.Settings.Alter()

#display new settings
$server.Settings
```

Once the script is done, you should be able to see the new value, as shown in the following screenshot:

```
AuditLevel               : All
BackupDirectory          : C:\Program Files\Microsoft SQL Server\MSSQL12.
DefaultFile              : C:\Program Files\Microsoft SQL Server\MSSQL12.
DefaultLog               : C:\Program Files\Microsoft SQL Server\MSSQL12.
LoginMode                : Integrated
MailProfile              :
NumberOfLogFiles         : -1
PerfMonMode              : None
TapeLoadWaitTime         : -1
Parent                   : [ROGUE]
OleDbProviderSettings    : {ADsDSOObject, MSDAOSP, MSDASQL, MSOLAP...}
Urn                      : Server[@Name='ROGUE']/Setting
Properties               : {Name=AuditLevel/Type=Microsoft.SqlServer.Mana
                           ue/Value=All,
                           Name=BackupDirectory/Type=System.String/Writak
                           Files\Microsoft SQL Server\MSSQL12.MSSQLSERVEF
                           Name=DefaultFile/Type=System.String/Writable=1
                           Files\Microsoft SQL Server\MSSQL12.MSSQLSERVEF
```

You can test this snippet using other configuration settings in your own instances. Usually, it is just a matter of giving the setting a new value and invoking the `Alter()` method.

Summary

In this chapter, we saw a number of snippets that allow us to scope out our SQL Server instance. A combination of WMI cmdlets and SMO script come in handy when using PowerShell to profile the instance and its environment. WMI can be quite helpful, especially when looking at system resources (such as CPU, memory, network, and disk space), while SMO is indispensable when programmatically listing or changing SQL Server properties. Using SMO, we saw how to list current instance settings, query SQL Server error logs, change service accounts, change audit-level settings, and adjust an instance's default backup directory property. This is just a glimpse of what you can do with SQL Server using PowerShell.

In the next chapter, we will look at how to do basic SQL Server administration tasks using PowerShell and SMO.

4
Basic SQL Server Administration

In this chapter, we will look at how to accomplish typical SQL Server administration tasks by using PowerShell. Although you were introduced to SQL Server-specific cmdlets in the previous chapters, these cmdlets are still quite few. Many of the tasks that we will see can be accomplished by using SQL **Server Management Objects** (**SMO**). As we encounter new SMO classes, it is best to verify the properties and methods of that class using Get-Help, or by directly visiting the TechNet or MSDN website.

The topics covered in this chapter include how to perform the following tasks:

- Listing databases and tables
- Adding files and filegroups
- Scripting database objects
- Attaching and detaching databases
- Backing up and restoring databases
- Reorganizing or rebuilding indexes
- Managing logins, users, and permissions
- Listing policies
- Managing jobs

Listing databases and tables

Let's start out by listing the current databases. The SMO Server class has access to all the databases in that instance, so a server variable will have to be created first. To create one using Windows Authentication, you can use the following snippet:

```
Import-Module SQLPS -DisableNameChecking


#current server name
$servername = "ROGUE"


#below should be a single line of code
$server = New-Object "Microsoft.SqlServer.Management.
  Smo.Server" $servername
```

If you need to use SQL Server Authentication, you can set the LoginSecure property to false, and prompt the user for the database credentials:

```
#with SQL authentication, we need
#to supply the SQL Login and password
$server.ConnectionContext.LoginSecure=$false;
$credential = Get-Credential
$server.ConnectionContext.set_Login($credential.UserName)
$server.ConnectionContext.set_SecurePassword($credential.Password)
```

Another way is to create a Microsoft.SqlServer.Management.Common.ServerConnection object and pass the database connection string:

```
#code below is a single line
$connectionString = "Server=$dataSource;uid=$username;
  pwd=$passwordd;Database=$database;Integrated Security=False"


$connection = New-Object System.Data.SqlClient.SqlConnection
$connection.ConnectionString = $connectionString
```

To find out how many databases are there, you can use the Count property of the Databases property:

```
$server.databases.Count
```

In addition to simply displaying the number of databases in an instance, we can also find out additional information such as creation data, recovery model, number of tables, stored procedures, and user-defined functions. The following is a sample script that pulls this information:

```
#create empty array
$result = @()
$server.Databases |
Where-Object IsSystemObject -eq $false |
ForEach-Object {
    $db = $_
    $object = [PSCustomObject] @{
        Name          = $db.Name
        CreateDate    = $db.CreateDate
        RecoveryModel = $db.RecoveryModel
        NumTables     = $db.Tables.Count
        NumUsers      = $db.Users.Count
        NumSP         = $db.StoredProcedures.Count
        NumUDF        = $db.UserDefinedFunctions.Count
    }
    $result += $object
}
$result |
Format-Table -AutoSize
```

A sample result looks like the following screenshot:

Name	CreateDate	RecoveryModel	NumTables	NumUsers	NumSP	NumUDF
Adventureworks2014	9/6/2014 2:01:44 PM	Simple	71	4	1393	122
AdventureworksLT2012	9/6/2014 2:03:14 PM	Simple	12	5	1385	114
Chinook	9/6/2014 1:58:21 PM	Full	11	4	1383	111
pubs	9/6/2014 1:58:12 PM	Full	11	4	1384	111

In this script, we have manipulated the output a little. Since we want information in a format different from the default, we created a custom object using the PSCustomObject class to store all this information. The PSCustomObject class was introduced in PowerShell V3.

You can also use `PSCustomObject` to draw data points from different objects and pull them together in a single result set. Each line in the sample result shown in the preceding screenshot is a single `PSCustomObject`. All of these, in turn, are stored in the `$result` array, which can be piped to the `Format-Table` cmdlet for a little easier display.

After learning these basics about `PSCustomObject`, you can adapt this script to increase the list of properties you are querying and change the formatting of the display. You can also export these to a file if you need to. We will use `PSCustomObject` a fair bit in the book, to create the output that we need.

To find out additional properties, you can pipe `$server.Databases` to the `Get-Member` cmdlet:

```
$server.Databases |
Get-Member |
Where-Object MemberType -eq "Property"
```

Once you execute this, your resulting screen should look similar to the following screenshot:

Name	MemberType	Definition
ActiveConnections	Property	int ActiveConnections {
ActiveDirectory	Property	Microsoft.SqlServer.Man
AnsiNullDefault	Property	bool AnsiNullDefault {g
AnsiNullsEnabled	Property	bool AnsiNullsEnabled {
AnsiPaddingEnabled	Property	bool AnsiPaddingEnabled
AnsiWarningsEnabled	Property	bool AnsiWarningsEnable
ApplicationRoles	Property	Microsoft.SqlServer.Man
ArithmeticAbortEnabled	Property	bool ArithmeticAbortEna
Assemblies	Property	Microsoft.SqlServer.Man
AsymmetricKeys	Property	Microsoft.SqlServer.Man
AutoClose	Property	bool AutoClose {get;set
AutoCreateIncrementalStatisticsEnabled	Property	bool AutoCreateIncremen
AutoCreateStatisticsEnabled	Property	bool AutoCreateStatisti
AutoShrink	Property	bool AutoShrink {get;se
AutoUpdateStatisticsAsync	Property	bool AutoUpdateStatisti
AutoUpdateStatisticsEnabled	Property	bool AutoUpdateStatisti
AvailabilityDatabaseSynchronizationState	Property	Microsoft.SqlServer.Man
AvailabilityGroupName	Property	string AvailabilityGrou
BrokerEnabled	Property	bool BrokerEnabled {get
CaseSensitive	Property	bool CaseSensitive {get
Certificates	Property	Microsoft.SqlServer.Man
ChangeTrackingAutoCleanUp	Property	bool ChangeTrackingAuto

To find out which methods are available for SMO database objects, we can use a very similar snippet, but this time, we will filter based on methods:

```
$server.Databases |
Get-Member |
Where-Object MemberType -eq "Method"
```

Once you execute this, your resulting screen should look similar to the following screenshot:

```
Name                        MemberType  Definition
----                        ----------  ----------
Alter                       Method      void Alter(), void Alter(Microsoft.S
ChangeMirroringState        Method      void ChangeMirroringState(Microsoft.
CheckAllocations            Method      System.Collections.Specialized.Strin
CheckAllocationsDataOnly    Method      System.Collections.Specialized.Strin
CheckCatalog                Method      System.Collections.Specialized.Strin
CheckIdentityValues         Method      void CheckIdentityValues()
Checkpoint                  Method      void Checkpoint()
CheckTables                 Method      System.Collections.Specialized.Strin
CheckTablesDataOnly         Method      System.Collections.Specialized.Strin
Create                      Method      void Create(bool forAttach), void Cr
Deny                        Method      void Deny(Microsoft.SqlServer.Manage
DisableAllPlanGuides        Method      void DisableAllPlanGuides()
Discover                    Method      System.Collections.Generic.List[Syst
Drop                        Method      void Drop(), void IDroppable.Drop()
DropAllPlanGuides           Method      void DropAllPlanGuides()
DropBackupHistory           Method      void DropBackupHistory()
EnableAllPlanGuides         Method      void EnableAllPlanGuides()
EnumBackupSetFiles          Method      System.Data.DataTable EnumBackupSetF
EnumBackupSets              Method      System.Data.DataTable EnumBackupSets
EnumCandidateKeys           Method      System.Data.DataTable EnumCandidateK
EnumDatabasePermissions     Method      Microsoft.SqlServer.Management.Smo.D
EnumLocks                   Method      System.Data.DataTable EnumLocks(int
EnumLoginMappings           Method      System.Data.DataTable EnumLoginMappi
EnumMatchingSPs             Method      Microsoft.SqlServer.Management.Smo.U
EnumObjectPermissions       Method      Microsoft.SqlServer.Management.Smo.O
```

Listing database files and filegroups

Managing databases also incorporates monitoring and managing of the files and filegroups associated with these databases. Still, using SMO, we can pull this information via PowerShell.

You can start by pulling all non-system databases:

```
$server.Databases |
Where-Object IsSystemObject -eq $false
```

The preceding snippet iterates over all the databases in the system. You can use the Foreach-Object cmdlet to do the iteration, and for each iteration, you can get a handle to the current database object. The SMO database object will have access to a Filegroups property, which you can query to find out more about the filegroups associated with each database:

```
ForEach-Object {
  $db = $_
  $db.FileGroups
}
```

This `FileGroups` class, in turn, can access all the files in that specific filegroup.

Here is the complete script that lists all files and filegroups for all databases. Note that we use `Foreach-Object` several times: once to loop through all databases, then to loop through all filegroups for each database, and again to loop through all files in each filegroup:

```
Import-Module SQLPS -DisableNameChecking

#current server name
$servername = "ROGUE"

$server = New-Object "Microsoft.SqlServer.Management.Smo.
  Server" $servername

$result = @()

$server.Databases |
Where-Object IsSystemObject -eq $false |
ForEach-Object {
    $db = $_
    $db.FileGroups |
    ForEach-Object {
        $fg = $_
        $fg.Files |
        ForEach-Object {
            $file = $_

            $object = [PSCustomObject] @{
                Database = $db.Name
                FileGroup = $fg.Name
                FileName = $file.FileName | Split-Path -Leaf
                "Size(MB)" = "{0:N2}" -f ($file.Size/1024)
                "UsedSpace(MB)" = "{0:N2}" -f ($file.UsedSpace/1MB)
                }
            $result += $object

        }
```

```
    }
}
$result |

Format-Table -AutoSize
```

A sample result looks like the following screenshot:

```
Database                FileGroup FileName                         Size(MB) UsedSpace(MB)
--------                --------- --------                         -------- -------------
AdventureWorks2014      PRIMARY   AdventureWorks2014_Data.mdf      205.25   0.18
AdventureWorksLT2012    PRIMARY   AdventureWorksLT2012_Data.mdf    8.31     0.01
Chinook                 PRIMARY   Chinook.mdf                      5.19     0.00
pubs                    PRIMARY   pubs.mdf                         3.19     0.00
Registration            DATA      data1.ndf                        4.00     0.00
Registration            DATA      data2.ndf                        4.00     0.00
Registration            PRIMARY   Registration.mdf                 4.00     0.00
Registration            READONLY  data3.ndf                        4.00     0.00
```

We have adjusted the result to make the display a bit more readable. For the `FileName` property, we extracted just the actual filename and did not report the path by piping the `FileName` property to the `Split-Path` cmdlet. The `-Leaf` option provides the filename part of the full path:

```
$file.FileName | Split-Path -Leaf
```

With `Size` and `UsedSpace`, we report the value in **megabytes (MB)**. Since the default sizes are reported in **kilobytes (KB)**, we have to divide the value by 1024. We also display the values with two decimal places:

```
"Size(MB)" = "{0:N2}" -f ($file.Size/1024)
"UsedSpace(MB)" = "{0:N2}" -f ($file.UsedSpace/1MB)
```

If you simply want to get the directory where the primary datafile is stored, you can use the following command:

```
$db.PrimaryFilePath
```

If you want to export the results to Excel or CSV, you simply need to take `$result` and instead of piping it to `Format-Table`, use one of the `Export` or `Convert` cmdlets.

Adding files and filegroups

Filegroups in SQL Server allow for a group of files to be managed together. It is almost akin to having folders on your desktop to allow you to manage, move, and save files together.

To add a filegroup, you have to use the `Microsoft.SqlServer.Management.Smo.Filegroup` class. Assuming you already have variables that point to your server instance, you can create a variable that references the database you wish to work with, as shown in the following snippet:

```
$dbname = "Registration"
$db = $server.Databases[$dbname]
```

Instantiating a `Filegroup` variable requires the handle to the SMO database object and a filegroup name. We have shown this in the following screenshot:

```
#code below is a single line
$fg = New-Object "Microsoft.SqlServer.Management.Smo.
  Filegroup" $db, "FG1"
```

When you're ready to create, invoke the `Create()` method:

```
$fg.Create()
```

Adding a datafile uses a similar approach. You need to identify which filegroup this new datafile belongs to. You will also need to identify the logical filename and actual file path of the new file. The following snippet will help you do that:

```
#code below is a single line
$datafile = New-Object "Microsoft.SqlServer.Management.Smo.DataFile" $fg,
"data4"

$datafile.FileName = "C:\DATA\data4.ndf"
$datafile.Create()
```

You can verify the changes visually in **SQL Server Management Studio** when you go to the database's properties. Under **Files**, you will see that the new secondary file, `data4.ndf`, has been added:

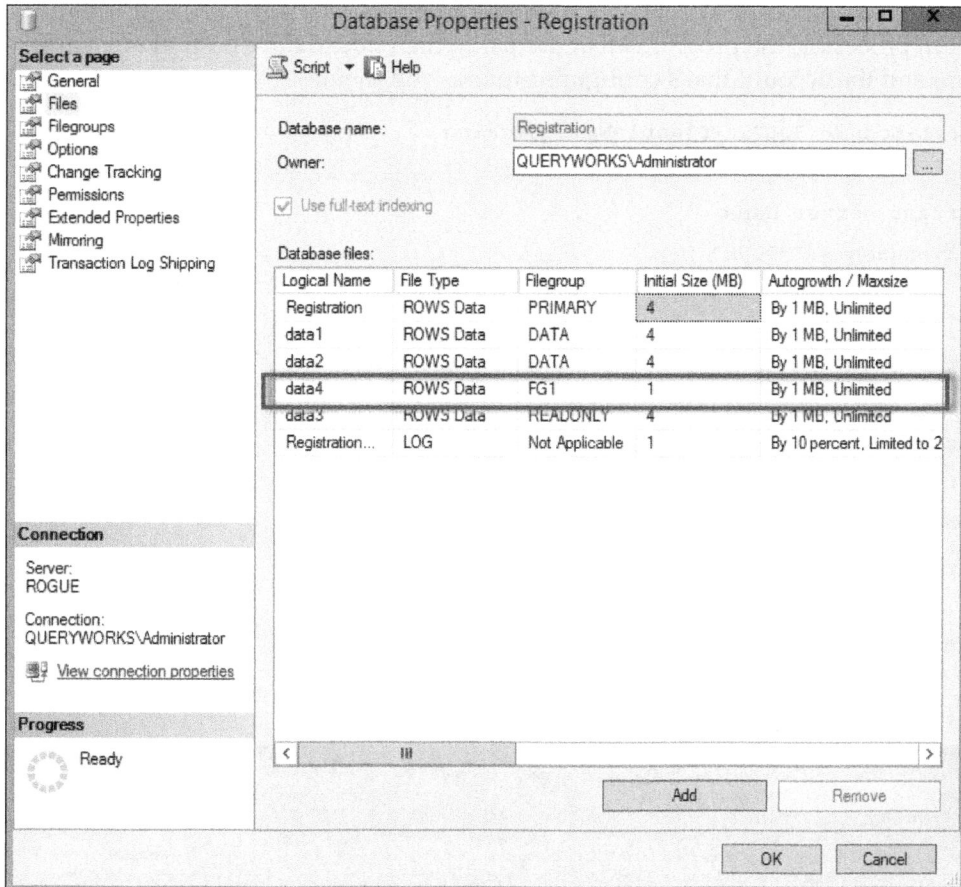

If, at a later time, you need to increase any of the files' sizes, you can use SMO to create a handle to the file and change the `Size` property. The `Size` property is allocated by KB, so you will need to calculate accordingly. After the `Size` property is changed, invoke the `Alter()` method to persist the changes. The following is an example snippet to do this:

```
$db = $server.Databases[$dbname]
$fg = $db.FileGroups["FG1"]
$file = $fg.Files["data4"]
$file.Size = 2 * 1024 #2MB
$file.Alter()
```

Listing the processes

SQL Server has a number of processes in the background that are needed for a normal operation. The SMO server class can access the list of processes by using the method `EnumProcesses()`. The following is an example script to pull current non-system processes, the programs that are using them, the databases that are using them, and the account that's configured to use/run them:

```
Import-Module SQLPS -DisableNameChecking


#current server name
$servername = "ROGUE"


$server = New-Object "Microsoft.SqlServer.Management.Smo.Server"
$servername


$server.EnumProcesses() |
Where-Object IsSystem -eq $false |
Select-Object Spid, Database,
IsSystem, Login, Status,
Cpu, MemUsage, Program |
Format-Table -AutoSize
```

The result that you will get looks like the following screenshot:

```
Spid Database IsSystem Login                        Status  Cpu MemUsage Program
---- -------- -------- -----                        ------  --- -------- -------
  51 msdb     False    QUERYWORKS\sqlservice                 16        2 SQLAgent - Job ...
  52 master   False    QUERYWORKS\Administrator running       0        0 SQL Management
  56 msdb     False    QUERYWORKS\sqlservice                172        2 SQLAgent - Gene...
  58 msdb     False    QUERYWORKS\sqlservice                  0        2 SQLAgent - Emai...
```

You can adjust this script based on your needs. For example, if you only need running queries, you can pipe it to the `Where-Object` cmdlet and filter by status. You can also sort the result based on the highest CPU or memory usage by piping this to the `Sort-Object` cmdlet.

Should you need to kill any process, for example when some processes are blocked, you can use the `KillProcess()` method of the SMO server object. You will need to pass the SQL Server session ID (or SPID) to this method:

```
$server.KillProcess($blockingSpid)
```

If you want to kill all processes in a specific database, you can use the `KillAllProcesses()` method and pass the database name:

```
$server.KillAllProcesses($dbname)
```

> Be careful though. Killing processes should not be done lightly. Before you kill a process, investigate what the process does, why you need to kill it, and what potential effects killing it will have on your database. Otherwise, killing processes could result in varying levels of system instability.

Checking enabled features

SQL has many features. We can find out if certain features are enabled by using SMO and PowerShell. To determine this, you need to access the object that owns that feature. For example, some features are available to be queried once you create an SMO server object:

```
Import-Module SQLPS -DisableNameChecking


#current server name
$servername = "ROGUE"


$server = New-Object "Microsoft.SqlServer.Management.Smo.Server"
$servername


$server |
Select-Object IsClustered, ClusterName,
FilestreamLevel,
IsFullTextInstalled,
LinkedServers,
IsHadrEnabled,
AvailabilityGroups
```

In the preceding script, we can easily find out the following parameters:

- Is the server clustered (`IsClustered`)?
- Does it support `FileStream` and to what level (`FilestreamLevel`)?
- Is `FullText` installed (`IsFullTextInstalled`)?
- Are there any configured linked servers in the system (`LinkedServers`)?
- Is `AlwaysOn` enabled (`IsHadrEnabled`) and are any availability groups configured (`AvailabilityGroups`)?

There are also a number of cmdlets available with the SQLPS module that allow you to manage the AlwaysOn parameter:

CommandType	Name	ModuleName
Cmdlet	Add-SqlAvailabilityDatabase	SQLPS
Cmdlet	Add-SqlAvailabilityGroupListenerStaticIp	SQLPS
Cmdlet	Join-SqlAvailabilityGroup	SQLPS
Cmdlet	New-SqlAvailabilityGroup	SQLPS
Cmdlet	New-SqlAvailabilityGroupListener	SQLPS
Cmdlet	New-SqlAvailabilityReplica	SQLPS
Cmdlet	Remove-SqlAvailabilityDatabase	SQLPS
Cmdlet	Remove-SqlAvailabilityGroup	SQLPS
Cmdlet	Remove-SqlAvailabilityReplica	SQLPS
Cmdlet	Resume-SqlAvailabilityDatabase	SQLPS
Cmdlet	Set-SqlAvailabilityGroup	SQLPS
Cmdlet	Set-SqlAvailabilityGroupListener	SQLPS
Cmdlet	Set-SqlAvailabilityReplica	SQLPS
Cmdlet	Suspend-SqlAvailabilityDatabase	SQLPS
Cmdlet	Switch-SqlAvailabilityGroup	SQLPS
Cmdlet	Test-SqlAvailabilityGroup	SQLPS
Cmdlet	Test-SqlAvailabilityReplica	SQLPS

> Replication can also be managed programmatically using the Replication Management Objects assembly. More information can be found at http://msdn.microsoft.com/en-us/library/ms146869.aspx.

Scripting database objects

Being able to script database objects is a powerful capability. There may be times when you'll need to have scripts handy, whether for versioning purposes or simply to provide them to your developers.

SMO largely drives this scripting capability. There is a class called Microsoft. SqlServer.Management.Smo.Scripter, which can be passed a collection of SMO objects to script:

```
$script.Script($smoObjects)
```

For example, if you need to script all stored procedures, you can add all the stored procedures into an array and pass this array to the Scripter object. You need to ensure that you are passing the actual stored procedure object and not just the names.

The `Scripter` object also accepts `ScriptingOptions`. There are a number of options that can be set. They include the following options:

- `DriAll`
- `DriIndexes`
- `DriNonClustered`
- `DriPrimaryKey`
- `DriUniqueKeys`
- `Encoding`
- `SchemaQualify`
- `ScriptDrops`
- `ScriptOwner`

> The complete documentation for all properties that can be set using the `ScriptingOptions` object can be found at http://msdn.microsoft.com/en-us/library/microsoft.sqlserver.management.smo.scriptingoptions_properties.aspx.

The following is an example snippet on how you can script all table objects for a particular database and save the script to a file:

```
Import-Module SQLPS -DisableNameChecking

#current server name
$servername = "ROGUE"

$server = New-Object "Microsoft.SqlServer.Management.Smo.
  Server" $servername

$dbname = "Chinook"
$db = $server.Databases[$dbname]

$script = New-Object "Microsoft.SqlServer.Management.Smo.
  Scripter" $server
$scriptOptions = New-Object "Microsoft.SqlServer.Management.Smo.
  ScriptingOptions"
$scriptOptions.AllowSystemObjects = $false
$scriptOptions.DriAll = $true
```

```
$scriptOptions.ToFileOnly = $true
$script.Options = $scriptOptions


$smoObjects = @()
$filename = "C:\DATA\$($dbname)_tables_export.sql"
$script.Options.FileName = $filename


$db.Tables |
Where-Object IsSystemObject -eq $false |
Foreach-Object {
    $smoObjects += $_
}
$script.Script($smoObjects)
```

Your file will contain the T-SQL statements required to recreate your tables:

```
Chinook_tables_export - Notepad
File  Edit  Format  View  Help
SET ANSI_NULLS ON
GO
SET QUOTED_IDENTIFIER ON
GO
CREATE TABLE [dbo].[Album](
        [AlbumId] [int] NOT NULL,
        [Title] [nvarchar](160) COLLATE SQL_Latin1_General_CP1_CI_AS NOT NULL,
        [ArtistId] [int] NOT NULL,
 CONSTRAINT [PK_Album] PRIMARY KEY CLUSTERED
(
        [AlbumId] ASC
)WITH (PAD_INDEX = OFF, STATISTICS_NORECOMPUTE = OFF, IGNORE_DUP_KEY = OFF, ALLOW_ROW_
) ON [PRIMARY]

GO
SET ANSI_NULLS ON
GO
SET QUOTED_IDENTIFIER ON
GO
CREATE TABLE [dbo].[Artist](
        [ArtistId] [int] NOT NULL,
        [Name] [nvarchar](120) COLLATE SQL_Latin1_General_CP1_CI_AS NULL,
 CONSTRAINT [PK_Artist] PRIMARY KEY CLUSTERED
(
        [ArtistId] ASC
)WITH (PAD_INDEX = OFF, STATISTICS_NORECOMPUTE = OFF, IGNORE_DUP_KEY = OFF, ALLOW_ROW_
```

Should you want to script out all stored procedures, for example, all you need to do is store all the stored procedures in the `$smoObjects` array and pass this to the `Script()` method:

```
$smoObjects = @()
$filename = "C:\DATA\$($dbname)_sp_export.sql"
$script.Options.FileName = $filename
$db.StoredProcedures |
Where-Object IsSystemObject -eq $false |
Foreach-Object {
    $smoObjects += $_
}
$script.Script($smoObjects)
```

If you need to copy the whole database using SMO, you can use the `Microsoft.SqlServer.Management.SMO.Transfer` class. To instantiate this, you are required to pass in an SMO database object along with the database you want to copy:

```
#code below is a single line
$transfer = New-Object -TypeName Microsoft.SqlServer.Management.SMO.
Transfer -ArgumentList $sourcedatabase
```

This SMO Transfer object has a number of option properties attached to it, similar to what you can find in the `ScriptingOptions` class. Once you've set your options, you can create just the script that transfers the database objects by using the `ScriptTransfer()` method, or you can choose to do the actual transfer, including data, using the `TransferData()` method. You can learn more about the SMO transfer class at http://msdn.microsoft.com/en-us/library/microsoft.sqlserver.management.smo.transfer.aspx.

Be careful about copying whole databases via SMO scripting, though. This could place a lot of load in your source system, especially when you are dealing with databases that have a lot of objects and/or data.

Attaching and detaching databases

Attaching and detaching databases can also be done programmatically using SMO. The SMO server object provides methods that allow you to perform this task quite simply.

Detaching databases

Before you detach a database, you must first check for a few conditions that might prevent the database from being detached. For example, if the database is currently being replicated or if the database has some existing snapshots, the database cannot be detached. Once these conditions are cleared, you can use the `DetachDatabase()` method to detach the database. The following is an example snippet:

```
Import-Module SQLPS -DisableNameChecking


#current server name

$sourcename = "ROGUE"

$sourceserver = New-Object "Microsoft.SqlServer.Management.Smo.Server"
$sourcename


$dbname = "Chinook"

$sourceserver.DetachDatabase($dbname, $true, $true)
```

Once this script has executed, you can confirm in SSMS whether the database has indeed been detached from the instance. Attaching the database requires a few more steps than detaching it. Firstly, you will need to check what files are required before you can attach and copy these files to your destination folder or server. In many cases, you will have more than just the primary datafile to attach. If you already know which files need to be attached, you can certainly hardcode each of those files in your script. However, it would be ideal if we can extract this information instead.

To find out which files are involved, you can pass the current `mdf` file to the `EnumDetachedDatabaseFiles()` and `EnumDetachedLogFiles()` methods:

```
$sourceserver.EnumDetachedDatabaseFiles($mdf)
$sourceserver.EnumDetachedLogFiles($mdf)
```

These methods will identify all data and logfiles related to the `mdf` file. You will need to store all of the file information that these two methods return in a `StringCollection` object. This collection can, in turn, be passed to the `AttachDatabase()` method of the SMO server object to complete the database attachment. The following is an example script that accomplishes the task:

```
Import-Module SQLPS -DisableNameChecking


#current server name

$destinationname = "ROGUE\SQL2014"
```

```
$destinationserver = New-Object "Microsoft.SqlServer.Management.Smo.
Server" $destinationname
$destinationserver.Name


$dbname = "Chinook"
$mdf = "C:\DATA\Chinook.mdf"


#this is where we will store all primary, secondary
#and log file information
$files = New-Object System.Collections.Specialized.StringCollection


#assuming we need the attach process to point to
#a different path than what's stored in the mdf
#we can specify a data path, and rebuild all the
#paths before we store in our collection
$datapath = "C:\DATA"


#collect all data file information
$sourceserver.EnumDetachedDatabaseFiles($mdf) |
ForEach-Object {
    #update location of file to new path
    $newfile = Join-Path $datapath (Split-Path $_ -Leaf)
    $files.Add($newfile)
}


#collect all log file information
$destinationserver.EnumDetachedLogFiles($mdf) |
ForEach-Object {
    #update location of file to new path
    $newfile = Join-Path $datapath (Split-Path $_ -Leaf)
    $files.Add($newfile)
}
$destinationserver.AttachDatabase($dbname, $files)
```

A number of options are also available to attach `AttachOptions`, which you can pass to the `AttachDatabase()` method. If you are using the ISE, an autocomplete dropdown appears once you type in `[Microsoft.SqlServer.Management.Smo.AttachOptions]::`, and it allows you to choose which options you need when attaching your database:

```
$dbowner = "QUERYWORKS\gon"
$destinationserver.AttachDatabase($dbname, $files, $dbowner,
[Microsoft.SqlServer.Management.Smo.AttachOptions]::|
```

EnableBroker
ErrorBrokerConversations
NewBroker
None
RebuildLog
Equals
Format
GetName
GetNames

Backing up and restoring databases

Backing up and restoring can be accomplished using **SQL Server Management Objects (SMO)** or by using the cmdlets available in the SQLPS module. As there are cmdlets available, in this section, we will focus on how to use these cmdlets.

Backing up

The `Backup-SqlDatabase` cmdlet that comes with the SQLPS modules allows you to perform database backups using different options. When you run `Get-Help Backup-SqlDatabase`, you should get a full list of syntax and examples. The options you get with this cmdlet are similar to the options you have with the BACKUP DATABASE T-SQL command. The following is an example script that performs a full database backup on a timestamped backup file:

```
Import-Module SQLPS -DisableNameChecking


#current server name
$servername = "ROGUE"


#$server = New-Object "Microsoft.SqlServer.Management.Smo.
  Server" $servername
```

```
$dbname = "Chinook"
$currdate = Get-Date -Format yyyyMMddHHmmss
$backupfolder = "C:\BACKUP\"


#generate backup file path and name
$fullbackupfilename = "$($dbname)_Full_$($currdate).bak"
$fullbackupfile = Join-Path $backupfolder $fullbackupfilename


#example filename that gets generated is:
#C:\BACKUP\Chinook_Full_20141023235306.bak


Backup-SqlDatabase -ServerInstance $servername
  -Database $dbname -BackupFile $fullbackupfile -Checksum
  -Initialize -BackupSetName "$dbname Full Backup"


Write-Output "Database has been backed up $fullbackupfile"
```

Creating a differential backup using the `Backup-SqlDatabase` cmdlet is not much different from a full backup, with the exception of the `-Incremental` option:

```
$diffbackupfilename = "$($dbname)_Diff_$($currdate).bak"
$diffbackupfile = Join-Path $backupfolder $diffbackupfilename


Backup-SqlDatabase -ServerInstance $servername -Database $dbname -
  BackupFile $diffbackupfile -Incremental -Checksum -Initialize -
  BackupSetName "$dbname Diff Backup"


Write-Output "Database has been backed up $diffbackupfile"
```

A transaction log backup requires a different `BackupAction` value:

```
$logbackupfilename = "$($dbname)_Log_$($currdate).trn"
$logbackupfile = Join-Path $backupfolder $logbackupfilename


Backup-SqlDatabase -ServerInstance $servername -Database $dbname -
  BackupFile $logbackupfile -BackupAction Log -Checksum -Initialize -
  BackupSetName "$dbname Txn Backup"


Write-Output "Database has been backed up $logbackupfile"
```

The `Backup-SqlDatabase` cmdlet also supports the `-Script` option, which generates the T-SQL equivalent of the backup command that you have specified. The following example displays this:

```
Backup-SqlDatabase -ServerInstance $servername -Database $dbname -
  BackupFile $logbackupfile -BackupAction Log -Checksum -Initialize -
  BackupSetName "$dbname Txn Backup" -Script
```

The preceding script will display the following output:

```
BACKUP LOG [Chinook] TO  DISK =
  N'C:\BACKUP\Chinook_Log_20141023235841.trn' WITH NOFORMAT, INIT,
  NAME = N'Chinook Txn Backup', NOSKIP, REWIND, NOUNLOAD,  STATS =
  10, CHECKSUM
GO
```

To check the backup sets in a backup file, similar to what RESTORE HEADERONLY does in T-SQL, you have to use an SMO restore object. It supports some methods that pull the backup metadata. You will have to add the files to the SMO `Restore` object using the `AddDevice()` method:

```
$restore.Devices.AddDevice($backupfile,
  [Microsoft.SqlServer.Management.Smo.DeviceType]::File)
```

The following is an example script that retrieves the backup header information:

```
Import-Module SQLPS -DisableNameChecking


#current server name
$servername = "ROGUE"


$server = New-Object "Microsoft.SqlServer.Management.Smo.
  Server" $servername


$dbname = "Chinook"
$restore = New-Object "Microsoft.SqlServer.Management.Smo.Restore"
$backupfile = "C:\BACKUP\Chinook_Full_20141023235841.bak"
$restore.Devices.AddDevice($backupfile,
  [Microsoft.SqlServer.Management.Smo.DeviceType]::File)
$restore.ReadBackupHeader($server)
```

The result of the preceding script looks like the following screenshot:

```
BackupName             : Chinook Full Backup
BackupDescription      :
BackupType             : 1
ExpirationDate         :
Compressed             : 0
Position               : 1
DeviceType             : 2
UserName               : QUERYWORKS\Administrator
ServerName             : ROGUE
DatabaseName           : Chinook
DatabaseVersion        : 782
DatabaseCreationDate   : 10/20/2014 9:42:09 PM
BackupSize             : 5059584
FirstLSN               : 95000000004500037
LastLSN                : 95000000006200001
CheckpointLSN          : 95000000004500037
DatabaseBackupLSN      : 95000000001800037|
BackupStartDate        : 10/23/2014 11:58:41 PM
BackupFinishDate       : 10/23/2014 11:58:41 PM
SortOrder              : 52
CodePage               : 0
UnicodeLocaleId        : 1033
UnicodeComparisonStyle : 196609
CompatibilityLevel     : 120
SoftwareVendorId       : 4608
SoftwareVersionMajor   : 12
SoftwareVersionMinor   : 0
SoftwareVersionBuild   : 2000
MachineName            : ROGUE
```

If you want to check out the file list, you can use the following command:

```
$restore.ReadFileList($server) |
Select Type, LogicalName, PhysicalName, FileGroupName, Size
```

This will give you the files involved in that database backup, as shown in the following screenshot:

```
Type          : D
LogicalName   : Chinook
PhysicalName  : C:\Program Files\Microsoft SQL Server\MSSQL12.MSSQLSE
FileGroupName : PRIMARY
Size          : 5439488

Type          : L
LogicalName   : Chinook_log
PhysicalName  : C:\Program Files\Microsoft SQL Server\MSSQL12.MSSQLSE
FileGroupName :
Size          : 851968
```

If you want to get the information about the media header, you can use the `ReadMediaHeader()` method:

```
$restore.ReadMediaHeader($server)
```

This will provide you with all the media metadata, as shown in the following screenshot:

```
MediaName               :
MediaSetId              : 023ec4a1-625d-46a5-9426-f7f0c8b92fa3
FamilyCount             : 1
FamilySequenceNumber    : 1
MediaFamilyId           : 0e0bedbe-0000-0000-0000-000000000000
MediaSequenceNumber     : 1
MediaLabelPresent       : 0
MediaDescription        :
SoftwareName            : Microsoft SQL Server
SoftwareVendorId        : 4608
MediaDate               : 10/23/2014 11:58:41 PM
MirrorCount             : 1
IsCompressed            : False
```

Restoring

As with the `Backup-SqlDatabase` cmdlet, the best way to get to know the `Restore-SqlDatabase` cmdlet is to use the `Get-Help` method. It supports a number of parameter sets, with options similar to the RESTORE DATABASE T-SQL command. Before you restore a database, you will need to find and figure out which database files you want to restore.

To restore a single full backup file, and leave the database in the `Restoring` state, you can use the following script as a reference:

```
Import-Module SQLPS -DisableNameChecking


#current server name
$servername = "ROGUE"
$dbname = "Chinook"


$backupfile = "C:\BACKUP\Chinook_Full_20141023235841.bak"
```

```
#code  below is a single line
Restore-SqlDatabase -Database $dbname -ReplaceDatabase -
  ServerInstance $servername -BackupFile $backupfile -NoRecovery
```

If the database files need to be relocated to a different folder, use the `-Relocate` file option. To restore a differential file on top of this `Chinook` database in the previous example, specify the differential backup file. If you plan to restore more transaction log backup files after this, you can keep the `-NoRecovery` option:

```
$backupfile = "C:\BACKUP\Chinook_Diff_20141023235841.bak"

Restore-SqlDatabase -Database $dbname -ReplaceDatabase -ServerInstance
$servername -BackupFile $backupfile -NoRecovery
```

To restore to a point in time, you can restore your transaction log backup file and specify the `-TopPointInTime` parameter:

```
$backupfile = "C:\BACKUP\Chinook_Log_20141023235841.trn"

Restore-SqlDatabase -Database $dbname -ReplaceDatabase -
  ServerInstance $servername -BackupFile $backupfile
  -ToPointInTime "2014-10-23 23:58:42"
```

If you are restoring multiple files, you will need to use the `Restore-SqlDatabase` cmdlet for each file, ensuring a `-NoRecovery` option until you have restored the last file. As you need to iterate over a number of files, you can integrate other PowerShell cmdlets such as `Get-ChildItem`, `Sort-Object`, and `Foreach-Object`:

```
Get-ChildItem $dir -Filter *.bak |
Sort-Object -Property CreationTime |
Foreach-Object{
    #do the restore here
}
```

Reorganizing or rebuilding indexes

Indexes are structures that can help speed up your queries. You can list all the indexes in your database tables and provide additional information such as the name, type, and fragmentation. To get all the indexes, you will have to get a handle to each table and access the `Indexes` property:

```
$table.Indexes
```

Each index, in turn, has its own methods and properties. Some properties that you may be interested in are Name, IndexType, Pages, FillFactor, PadIndex, and SpaceUsed. It also has a method EnumFragmentation(), which retrieves the current fragmentation value. Here is an example script to retrieve indexes and some properties, including fragmentation information:

```
Import-Module SQLPS -DisableNameChecking

#current server name
$servername = "ROGUE"

$server = New-Object "Microsoft.SqlServer.Management.Smo.
  Server" $servername
$dbname = "Chinook"

$result = @()

$db = $server.Databases[$dbname]
$db.Tables |
ForEach-Object {
    $table = $_
    $table.Indexes |
    Sort-Object -Property Name |
    ForEach-Object {
      $index = $_
      $frag = $index.EnumFragmentation()

      $object = [PSCustomObject] @{
          Table = $table.Name
          Index = $index.Name
          Type = $frag.IndexType
          Pages = $frag.Pages
          "AvgFragmentation %" = "{0:N2}" -f ($frag.AverageFragmentation)
          "SpaceUsed(KB)" = $index.SpaceUsed

    }
        $result += $object
    }
}
$result |
Format-Table
```

Your result will look similar to the following screenshot:

```
Table          Index                     Type                  Pages AvgFragmentation % SpaceUsed(KB)
-----          -----                     ----                  ----- ------------------ -------------
Album          IFK_AlbumArtistId         NONCLUSTERED INDEX        1 0.00                           16
Album          PK_Album                  CLUSTERED INDEX           3 33.33                          16
Artist         PK_Artist                 CLUSTERED INDEX           2 50.00                          16
Customer       IFK_CustomerSupportRepId  NONCLUSTERED INDEX        1 0.00                           16
Customer       PK_Customer               CLUSTERED INDEX           2 50.00                          16
Employee       IFK_EmployeeReportsTo     NONCLUSTERED INDEX        1 0.00                           16
Employee       PK_Employee               CLUSTERED INDEX           1 0.00                            8
Genre          PK_Genre                  CLUSTERED INDEX           1 0.00                            8
Invoice        IFK_InvoiceCustomerId     NONCLUSTERED INDEX        1 0.00                           16
Invoice        PK_Invoice                CLUSTERED INDEX           7 14.29                          16
InvoiceLine    IFK_InvoiceLineInvoiceId  NONCLUSTERED INDEX        4 75.00                          48
InvoiceLine    IFK_InvoiceLineTrackId    NONCLUSTERED INDEX        5 80.00                          56
InvoiceLine    PK_InvoiceLine            CLUSTERED INDEX          10 30.00                          16
MediaType      PK_MediaType              CLUSTERED INDEX           1 0.00                            8
Playlist       PK_Playlist               CLUSTERED INDEX           1 0.00                            8
PlaylistTrack  IFK_PlaylistTrackTrackId  NONCLUSTERED INDEX       32 96.88                         272
PlaylistTrack  PK_PlaylistTrack          NONCLUSTERED INDEX       41 85.37                         344
Track          IFK_TrackAlbumId          NONCLUSTERED INDEX        9 88.89                          88
Track          IFK_TrackGenreId          NONCLUSTERED INDEX       11 90.91                         104
Track          IFK_TrackMediaTypeId      NONCLUSTERED INDEX        7 85.71                          72
```

After you identify the indexes, you might need to do some house cleaning by way of rebuilding or reorganizing your indexes. Typically, you consider fragmentation percentage with the number of pages. There are some rough guidelines, but your mileage might vary, so you should benchmark and see what numbers are right for your environment.

Let's assume you want to reorganize indexes if fragmentation is between 10 and 30 percent, and with at least 1000 pages. If fragmentation exceeds 30 percent and pages are at least 1000, you want to reorganize. The following snippet will help you accomplish this task:

```
#$indexFrag is an object resulting from EnumFragmentation()

if ($indexFrag.AverageFragmentation -ge 10 -and
   $indexFrag.AverageFragmentation -le 30 -and $indexFrag.Pages
   -ge 1000)
{
    $index.Reorganize()
}
elseif ($indexFrag.AverageFragmentation -ge 30 -and
   $indexFrag.Pages -ge 1000)
{
    $index.Rebuild()
}
```

Managing logins, users, and permissions

PowerShell and SMO can help pull a list of SQL Server logins, database users, and permissions. Since a login is an instance-level object, you can use the SMO Server object to pull information about every login registered in your instance. You can also list all the server roles this login belongs to, as shown in the following snippet:

```
Import-Module SQLPS -DisableNameChecking

#current server name
$servername = "ROGUE"

$server = New-Object "Microsoft.SqlServer.Management.Smo.Server"
$servername

$result = @()

$server.Logins |
Where-Object IsSystemObject -EQ $false |
ForEach-Object {
    $login = $_
    $object = [pscustomobject] @{
        Login = $login.Name
        LoginType = $login.LoginType
        CreateDate = $login.CreateDate
        ServerRoles = $login.ListMembers()
    }
    $result += $object
}
$result |
Format-Table -AutoSize
```

A sample output is provided in the following screenshot:

```
Login                              LoginType    CreateDate                ServerRoles
-----                              ---------    ----------                -----------
##MS_PolicyEventProcessingLogin##   SqlLogin    2/20/2014 8:49:46 PM      {}
##MS_PolicyTsqlExecutionLogin##     SqlLogin    2/20/2014 8:49:46 PM      {}
NT AUTHORITY\SYSTEM                 WindowsUser  8/21/2014 7:15:28 PM      {}
NT SERVICE\MSSQLSERVER              WindowsUser  8/21/2014 7:15:28 PM      {sysadmin}
NT SERVICE\SQLSERVERAGENT           WindowsUser  8/21/2014 7:15:28 PM      {sysadmin}
NT SERVICE\SQLWriter                WindowsUser  8/21/2014 7:15:27 PM      {sysadmin}
NT SERVICE\Winmgmt                  WindowsUser  8/21/2014 7:15:27 PM      {sysadmin}
QUERYWORKS\Administrator            WindowsUser  8/21/2014 7:15:27 PM      {sysadmin}
QUERYWORKS\gon                      WindowsUser  10/20/2014 12:04:11 PM    {serveradmin, setupadmin}
QUERYWORKS\killua                   WindowsUser  10/20/2014 12:04:31 PM    {dbcreator, bulkadmin}
sqlbelle                            SqlLogin     10/18/2014 8:02:10 AM     {}
sqlservice                          SqlLogin     10/23/2014 5:56:08 AM     {processadmin}
```

Each SMO login object also has access to additional methods such as `EnumCredentials()` and `EnumDatabaseMappings()`. To list all database users, we need to iterate over all the databases in the server or only in the database you want to query. An SMO user object has properties such as `Name`, `UserType`, `Login`, and `LoginType`, which will allow us to get all the database mappings. If you want to identify orphaned users in your database, simply check the `UserType` property. A value of `NoLogin` indicates an orphaned user:

```
Import-Module SQLPS -DisableNameChecking

#current server name
$servername = "ROGUE"

$server = New-Object "Microsoft.SqlServer.Management.Smo.
  Server" $servername

$result = @()
$server.Databases |
Where-Object IsSystemObject -EQ $false |
ForEach-Object {
    $db = $_
    $db.Users |
    Where-Object IsSystemObject -eq $false |
    ForEach-Object {
        $dbuser = $_
        $object = [PSCustomObject] @{
        Database = $db.Name
        DBUser = $dbuser.Name
        Orphaned = if ($dbUser.UserType -eq "NoLogin")
          {"Yes"} else {"No"}
```

```
        Login = $dbuser.Login
        LoginType = $dbUser.LoginType
        }
  $result += $object
    }
}
$result |
Format-Table -AutoSize
```

What you will get is the list of database users and the logins that they map to:

```
Database            DBUser                         Orphaned  Login                          LoginType
--------            ------                         --------  -----                          ---------
AdventureWorks2014  QUERYWORKS\killua              No        QUERYWORKS\killua              ...owsUser
AdventureWorksLT2012 NT AUTHORITY\NETWORK SERVICE  No        NT AUTHORITY\NETWORK SERVICE   ...owsUser
AdventureWorksLT2012 QUERYWORKS\gon                No        QUERYWORKS\gon                 ...owsUser
Chinook             QUERYWORKS\gon                No        QUERYWORKS\gon                 ...owsUser
Chinook             QUERYWORKS\killua              No        QUERYWORKS\killua              ...owsUser
pubs                QUERYWORKS\killua              No        QUERYWORKS\killua              ...owsUser
pubs                sqlbelle                       No        sqlbelle                       SqlLogin
pubs                wolverine                      Yes                                      SqlLogin
```

Permissions

It is also important to keep tabs of what permissions have been issued to your database users. Using the same Users property of your SMO database object, you can list the objects and permissions that have been issued, including the type, that is, grant, deny, or revoke:

```
Import-Module SQLPS -DisableNameChecking


#current server name
$servername = "ROGUE"
$dbname = "Chinook"


$server = New-Object "Microsoft.SqlServer.Management.Smo.
  Server" $servername


$result = @()
$server.Databases |
Where-Object IsSystemObject -EQ $false |
Where-Object Name -eq $dbname |
ForEach-Object {
    $db = $_
```

```
    $db.Users |
    Where-Object IsSystemObject -eq $false |
    ForEach-Object {
        $dbuser = $_

        $object = [PSCustomObject] @{
        Database = $db.Name
        DBUser = $dbuser.Name
        Orphaned = if ($dbUser.UserType -eq "NoLogin")
          {"Yes"} else {"No"}
        Login = $dbuser.Login
        LoginType = $dbUser.LoginType
        DBRoles = $dbuser.EnumRoles()
        ObjectPermissions  = ($db.EnumObjectPermissions
          ($dbuser.Name) | SELECT @{N="P";E={$_.ObjectName + " " +
          $_.PermissionState + " " + $_.PermissionType  }} )
        }
    $result += $object
    }
}
$result |
Format-List
```

What you will get will look similar to the following screenshot:

```
Database           : Chinook
DBUser             : sqlbelle
Orphaned           : No
Login              : sqlbelle
LoginType          : SqlLogin
DBRoles            : {db_ddladmin, db_datareader, db_datawriter}
ObjectPermissions  : {@{P=Album Grant ALTER}, @{P=Artist Grant DELETE},
                     @{P=Artist Grant SELECT}...}
```

We can improve the formatting of the object permissions. If we want, we can list the permissions for each database user by using the EnumObjectPermissions() method and piping the results to a Select-Object cmdlet. This will provide a tabular view of the permissions, one permission per line:

```
$db.EnumObjectPermissions($dbuser.Name) |
Select-Object ObjectName, PermissionState, PermissionType |
Format-Table -AutoSize
```

The result will look like the following screenshot:

```
ObjectName  PermissionState  PermissionType
----------  ---------------  --------------
Album                 Grant  ALTER
Artist                Grant  DELETE
Artist                Grant  INSERT
Artist                Grant  SELECT
vwAlbums              Grant  REFERENCES
vwAlbums              Grant  SELECT
vwAlbums              Grant  VIEW DEFINITION
```

Adding a login

A login is an instance-level principal. To access an instance's logins, we can use the SMO server variable. To add a new login using SMO, we have to first create a `Microsoft.SqlServer.Management.Smo.Login` object. We then have to identify what type of login it is. This can be specified using the `Microsoft.SqlServer.Management.Smo.LoginType` enumeration. There are five valid values, which are listed as follows:

- `AsymmetricKey`
- `Certificate`
- `SqlLogin`
- `WindowsGroup`
- `WindowsUser`

Anytime you need to enter the password, you can use the `Read-Host` cmdlet, so you don't have to hardcode it in your script. Instead, you are prompted on the fly. You can also use the `-AsSecureString` to mask the entered password. After you have all this information, you can call the login's `Create()` method. Here is an example script that adds a new SQL login called `kurapika`:

```
Import-Module SQLPS -DisableNameChecking

#current server name
$servername = "ROGUE"

$server = New-Object "Microsoft.SqlServer.Management.Smo.
  Server" $servername

$loginname = "kurapika"
```

```
#for this example, we will check if login exists
#and if it does we will drop it
if ($server.Logins.Contains($loginname))
{
    $server.Logins[$loginname].Drop()
}


$login = New-Object "Microsoft.SqlServer.Management.Smo.
  Login" $server, $loginname
$login.LoginType = [Microsoft.SqlServer.Management.Smo.LoginType]::
  SqlLogin
$login.PasswordExpirationEnabled = $false


#prompt for password
$password = Read-Host "Password: " -AsSecureString
$login.Create($password)
```

You can confirm this in **SQL Server Management Studio** by navigating to **Security | Logins**, or by re-running the prior script that lists the logins:

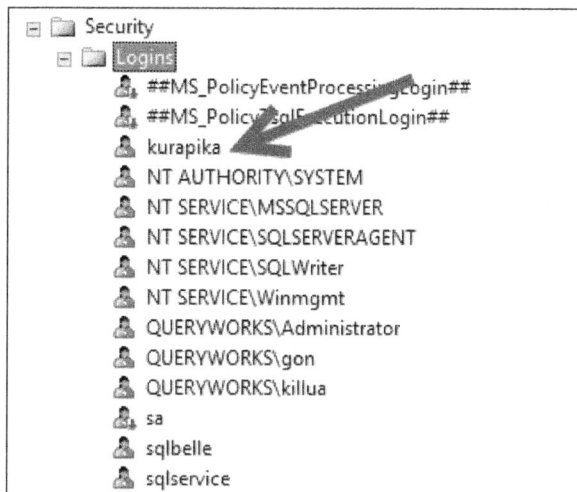

To add this login to a server-level role, you can use the `AddToRole()` method and specify the server role:

```
#add to server roles
$server.Logins[$loginname].AddToRole("dbcreator")
```

To confirm this in **SQL Server Management Studio**, open the login's properties and check the **Server Roles** page:

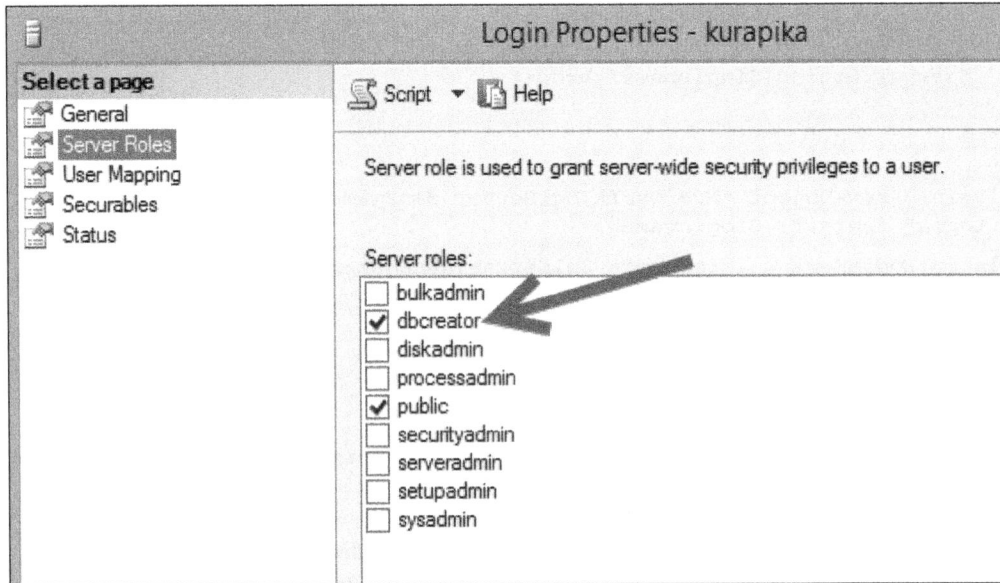

Adding database users

In addition to adding and managing logins, you can also add and manage database users using PowerShell and SMO using the `Microsoft.SqlServer.Management.Smo.User` object. A database user needs to be mapped to a valid login, which can be set using the `Login` property of the SMO user object. Similar to the login creation, once all this information has been provided, you can invoke the `Create()` method of the SMO user object to persist the changes:

```
#add database mapping
$dbname = "Chinook"
$dbusername = "kurapika"
$db = $server.Databases[$dbname]

if ($db.Users.Contains($dbusername))
{
    $db.Users[$dbusername].Drop()
}
```

```
$dbuser = New-Object "Microsoft.SqlServer.Management.Smo.
  User" $db, $dbusername
$dbuser.Login = $loginname
$dbuser.Create()
```

To confirm the task just performed in **SQL Server Management Studio**, go to the `Security` folder of the database you used, and confirm whether the user exists in the list:

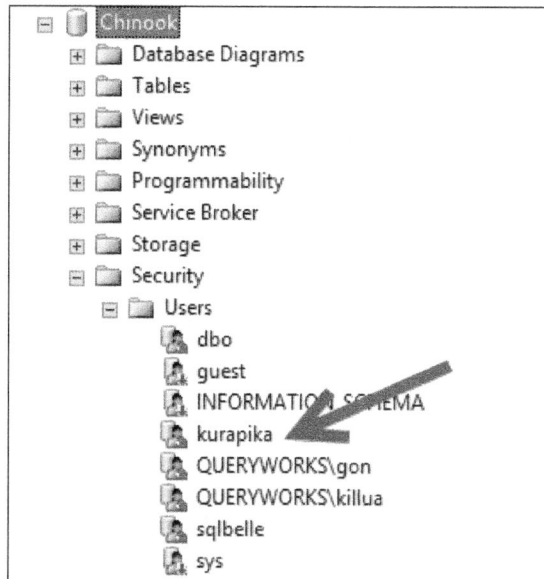

To add this database user to a database role, you can use the SMO database's `Roles` property to specify the database role and its `AddMember()` method to add the database user:

```
#add database role
$db.Roles["db_datareader"].AddMember($dbuser.Name)
```

You can confirm this change by opening the database user's properties in **SQL Server Management Studio** and going to the **Membership** page:

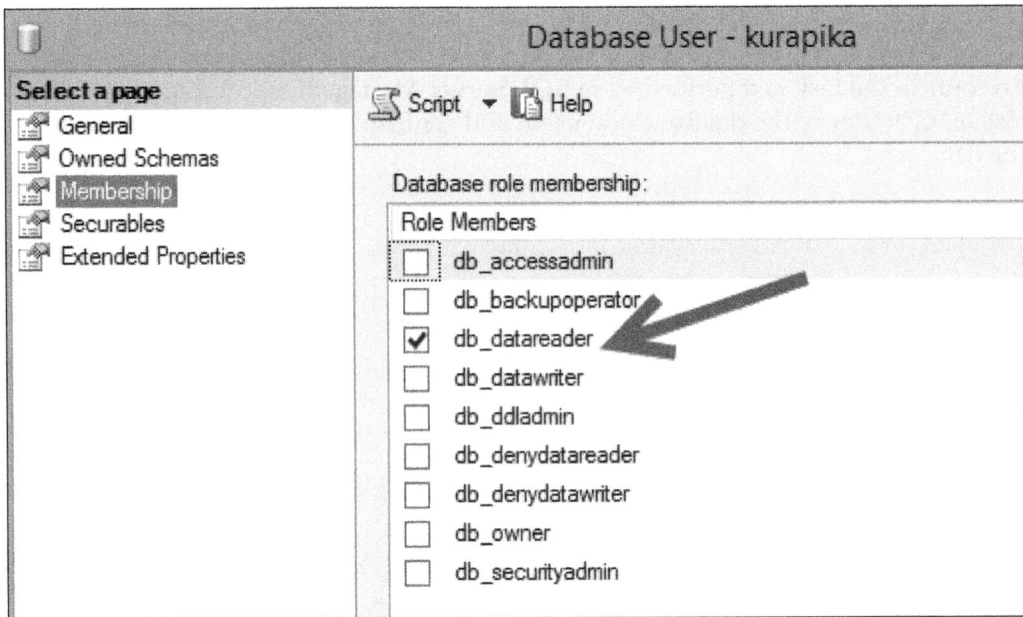

You can also assign specific permissions to your database users. This will require creating a `Microsoft.SqlServer.Management.Smo.ObjectPermissionSet` object and adding the specific permissions. The permission that you add has to be a valid `Microsoft.SqlServer.Management.Smo.ObjectPermission` enumeration value. You can check out all the permissible values from `http://msdn.microsoft.com/en-us/library/microsoft.sqlserver.management.smo.objectpermission.aspx`.

Once the permission is set up, you can use a specific database object's `Grant()`, `Deny()`, or `Revoke()` method to complete the assignment:

```
#initial permission is View Definition
$permissionset = New-Object "Microsoft.SqlServer.Management.Smo.
ObjectPermissionSet"
  ([Microsoft.SqlServer.Management.Smo.ObjectPermission]::
  ViewDefinition)


#add additional permission: Alter
$permissionset.Add([Microsoft.SqlServer.Management.Smo.
  ObjectPermission]::Alter)
```

```
#add permission set to the database view vwAlbums
$db.Views["vwAlbums"].Grant($permissionset, $dbuser.Name)
```

You can confirm this in **SQL Server Management Studio** by going to the database user's properties and checking out the **Securables** page:

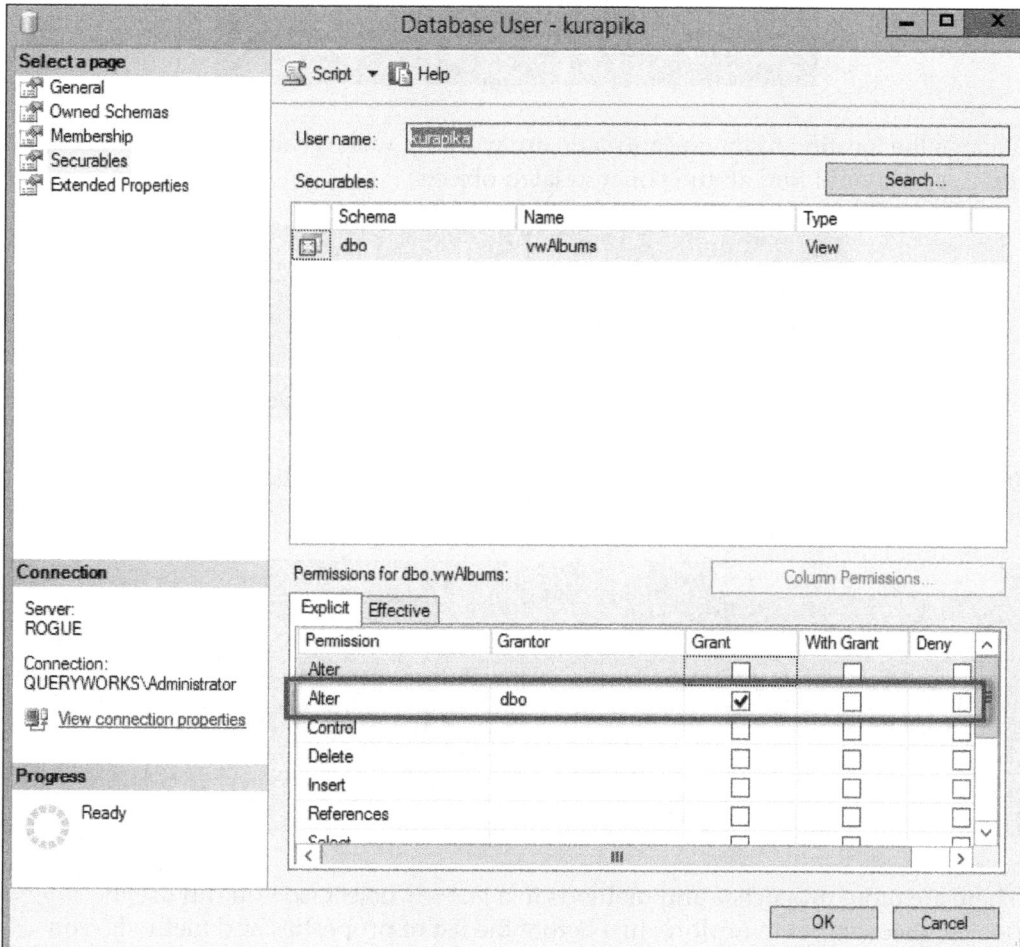

Policies

We can check out policies in a SQL Server instance as well, by using PowerShell. Instead of using SMO, we can use the SQLSERVER PSDrive. You can first change your location to the SQLPolicy node:

```
Set-Location "SQLSERVER:\SQLPolicy\YourSqlServerMachineName"
```

You can use `dir` or `Get-ChildItem` to navigate to the available instances:

```
PS SQLSERVER:\SQLPolicy\ROGUE> dir

Instance Name
-------------
DEFAULT
SQL2014
```

Change the location to the instance you are working with. When you list the current items, you should find all the policy-related objects:

```
PS SQLSERVER:\SQLPolicy\ROGUE\DEFAULT> dir
Conditions
ObjectSets
Policies
PolicyCategories
PolicyCategorySubscriptions
```

If you navigate to `Policies`, you will be able to see all the policies that are currently installed in the instance (if you have any already installed):

```
Name                          Category          Created              Enabled
----                          --------          -------              -------
CmdExec Rights Secured        Microsoft Best... 10/25/2014 9:14 PM   False
Database Auto Shrink          Microsoft Best... 10/25/2014 9:14 PM   False
Database Collation            Microsoft Best... 10/25/2014 9:14 PM   False
Guest Permissions             Microsoft Best... 10/25/2014 9:14 PM   False
Last Successful Backup Date   Microsoft Best... 10/25/2014 9:14 PM   False
SQL Server Login Mode         Microsoft Best... 10/25/2014 9:14 PM   False
SQL Server Password Expiration Microsoft Best... 10/25/2014 9:14 PM  False
SQL Server Password Policy    Microsoft Best... 10/25/2014 9:14 PM   False
Trustworthy Database          Microsoft Best... 10/25/2014 9:14 PM   False
```

There are more properties and methods to a `Policy` object, so you can use the `Get-Member` cmdlet to explore. Just before the list of properties and methods, you should also find that each policy is a `Microsoft.SqlServer.Management.Dmf.Policy` object. Knowing this information will enable you to work with policies programmatically, the same way we've used SMO in previous sections:

```
PS SQLSERVER:\SQLPolicy\ROGUE\DEFAULT\Policies> Get-ChildItem | Get-Member


    TypeName: Microsoft.SqlServer.Management.Dmf.Policy

Name                            MemberType   Definition
----                            ----------   ----------
ConnectionProcessingFinished    Event        ConnectionProcessingFinishedEven
ConnectionProcessingStarted     Event        ConnectionProcessingStartedEvent
PolicyEvaluationFinished        Event        PolicyEvaluationFinishedEventHan
PolicyEvaluationStarted         Event        PolicyEvaluationStartedEventHand
PropertyChanged                 Event        System.ComponentModel.PropertyCh
PropertyMetadataChanged         Event        System.EventHandler`1[Microsoft.
TargetProcessed                 Event        TargetProcessedEventHandler Targ
Alter                           Method       void Alter(), void IAlterable.Al
Create                          Method       void Create(), void ICreatable.C
Discover                        Method       void Discover(Microsoft.SqlServe
Drop                            Method       void Drop(), void IDroppable.Dro
Equals                          Method       bool Equals(System.Object obj)
Evaluate                        Method       bool Evaluate(Microsoft.SqlServe
GetDomain                       Method       Microsoft.SqlServer.Management.S
GetHashCode                     Method       int GetHashCode()
GetPropertySet                  Method       Microsoft.SqlServer.Management.S
GetType                         Method       type GetType()
ProduceConfigureScript          Method       string ProduceConfigureScript(Sy
```

To invoke a policy, you can use the `Invoke-PolicyEvaluation` cmdlet. While you are still in the `Policies` node, you can choose one or multiple policies and pipe them to the `Invoke-PolicyEvaluation` cmdlet:

```
Get-Item "Trustworthy Database" |
  Invoke-PolicyEvaluation -TargetServerName "ROGUE"
```

You should get immediate feedback as shown in the following screenshot after you execute the preceding line:

```
ID Policy Name            Result Start Date          End Date            Messages
-- -----------            ------ ----------          --------            --------
1 Trustworthy Database    True   10/25/2014 9:44 PM  10/25/2014 9:44 PM
```

Managing jobs

You can list information on the current job server and the related jobs. Once the SMO server is set up, you can list the properties by using the following command:

```
$server.JobServer | Select-Object *
```

A long list of properties will be displayed. A partial list looks like the following screenshot:

```
SaveInSentFolder          : False
ServiceAccount            : QUERYWORKS\sqlservice
ServiceStartMode          : Auto
SqlAgentAutoStart         : True
SqlAgentMailProfile       :
SqlAgentRestart           : True
SqlServerRestart          : True
WriteOemErrorLog          : False
Parent                    : [ROGUE]
Name                      : ROGUE
JobCategories             : {[Uncategorized (Local)], [Uncategorized (Multi-Server)], Data
                            Collector, Database Engine Tuning Advisor...}
OperatorCategories        : {[Uncategorized]}
AlertCategories           : {[Uncategorized], Replication}
AlertSystem               : [ROGUE]
Alerts                    : {}
Operators                 : {}
TargetServers             : {}
TargetServerGroups        : {}
Jobs                      : {Backup Database, Export Client Data, syspolicy_purge_history}
SharedSchedules           : {CollectorSchedule_Every_10min, CollectorSchedule_Every_15min,
                            CollectorSchedule_Every_30min, CollectorSchedule_Every_5min...}
ProxyAccounts             : {sharedfileuser}
SysAdminOnly              :
Urn                       : Server[@Name='ROGUE']/JobServer
Properties                : {Name=AgentLogLevel/Type=Microsoft.SqlServer.Management.Smo.Age
                            tLogLevels/Writable=True/Value=Errors, Warnings,
                            Name=AgentShutdownWaitTime/Type=System.Int32/Writable=True/Valu
                            Name=ErrorLogFile/Type=System.String/Writable=True/Value=C:\Pro
```

Notice that information on the job server includes the service account, job categories, alerts, operators, jobs, proxy accounts, and shared schedules.

To list details about the jobs, you can use the same `JobServer` object and iterate over all the jobs in that collection. Each SMO `Job` object contains information about the job name, last run date, last run outcome, and each step's individual outcome. A sample script that lists the job details is as follows:

```
Import-Module SQLPS -DisableNameChecking


#current server name
$servername = "ROGUE"        # or localhost


$server = New-Object "Microsoft.SqlServer.Management.Smo.Server"
$servername


$result = @()
```

```
$server.JobServer.Jobs |
Foreach-Object {
    $job = $_
    $job.JobSteps |
    ForEach-Object {
        $jobstep = $_
        $object = [PSCustomObject] @{
            Name = $job.Name
            LastRunDate = $job.LastRunDate
            LastRunOutcome = $job.LastRunOutcome
            Step = $jobstep.Name
            LastStepOutcome = $jobstep.LastRunOutcome
        }
        $result += $object
    }
}


$result |
Format-Table
```

Your result will look like the following screenshot:

```
Name                 LastRunDate          LastRunOutcome Step                    LastStepOutcome
----                 -----------          -------------- ----                    ---------------
Backup Database      10/23/2014 12:35...      Succeeded Step 1                        Succeeded
Export Client Data   10/23/2014 12:34...         Failed Step 1 - Use SSIS               Failed
syspolicy_purge_...  10/23/2014 2:00:...      Succeeded Verify that auto...         Succeeded
syspolicy_purge_...  10/23/2014 2:00:...      Succeeded Purge history.             Succeeded
syspolicy_purge_...  10/23/2014 2:00:...      Succeeded Erase Phantom Sy...        Succeeded
```

Should you want to display more columns, you might need to pass the $result variable to Format-List instead of Format-Table. Otherwise, Format-Table will not be able to display the complete details. Notice from the preceding screenshot that some fields have been truncated and replaced by multiple dots (...) to signify that they are incompletely displayed.

Summary

Many SQL Server administration tasks can be accomplished using PowerShell. In this chapter, we covered tasks ranging from listing databases and files, attaching and detaching databases, monitoring and managing logins and users, to checking jobs and invoking policies.

The SQLPS module comes with some cmdlets that can be used, for example `Backup-SqlDatabase` and `Restore-SqlDatabase`, as well as a number of cmdlets related to `AlwaysOn`. However, the number of cmdlets in SQLPS is still quite few. Often, accomplishing tasks more effectively via scripting will require you to use SMO, especially for tasks where appropriate cmdlets are not available.

In the next chapter, we will explore different ways to send queries to SQL Server via PowerShell.

5

Querying SQL Server with PowerShell

We can query SQL Server from within PowerShell. This chapter illustrates different ways in which we can send and execute queries in SQL Server using PowerShell, and also evaluate when it is appropriate to use this method to do the job.

The topics that will be covered in this chapter are as follows:

- To PowerShell or not to PowerShell
- Sending queries to SQL Server
- Fixing orphaned users
- Getting fragmentation data
- Backing up and restoring databases
- Exporting data using `bcp`

To PowerShell or not to PowerShell

The great debate is—why would you use PowerShell to send queries to SQL Server? This is a valid question. What is important to understand is that PowerShell is yet another tool that can help you perform certain tasks. However, by no means is PowerShell the only tool, nor is PowerShell the best tool for all cases.

As a rule of thumb, it is best to use native, set-based T-SQL statements when possible. When you use SMO or ADO.NET, be aware that you are adding one more layer of translation before the query gets to SQL Server, which may not always be efficient.

Running the T-SQL scripts from PowerShell could be useful, especially when it is part of a bigger PowerShell scripting solution. For example, it is useful if you are integrating this into an automation solution between SharePoint, Active Directory, Exchange, and SQL Server, like a script that automatically builds a SharePoint farm. Let's look at a few more cases.

Creating databases and tables would be simpler and faster if done directly in SQL Server, as with creating SQL Server Agent jobs or policies. If you wrap this in PowerShell code, you will end up with a lot of code, and perhaps be less efficient.

If you are sending queries to multiple servers, where the values for parameters are coming from a file, then PowerShell may be a good solution. If you are collecting metrics and exporting these to a file or even back to SQL Server, PowerShell may still be a good candidate.

Sending queries to SQL Server

Querying is a typical task we do with SQL Server. Normally we would open **SQL Server Management Studio** (**SSMS**) and type and execute our queries from there. If we are using PowerShell, that routine needs to be slightly adjusted. The few ways we can send queries to SQL Server using PowerShell are as follows:

- SQL **Server Management Objects** (**SMO**)
- `Invoke-Sqlcmd`
- ADO.NET
- `Invoke-Expression`

SQL Server Management Objects

We have been using SQL **Server Management Objects** (**SMO**) for a few chapters now. Although it's indirect, when we create SMO objects, use properties, and invoke methods, we are technically sending queries to SQL Server. Let us take the following snippet, for example:

```
$servername = "ROGUE"    # or localhost
$server = New-Object -TypeName Microsoft.SqlServer.Management.Smo.
Server -ArgumentList $servername

$dbname = "TestDB"
$db = New-Object -TypeName Microsoft.SqlServer.Management.Smo.
Database($server, $dbname)
$db.Create()
```

What we are really doing here is connecting to the instance ROGUE and sending a CREATE DATABASE statement to the server.

The Invoke-Sqlcmd cmdlet

The Invoke-Sqlcmd cmdlet allows you to send most types of queries to SQL Server. Invoke-Sqlcmd is the cmdlet equivalent to the sqlcmd utility, which is a lightweight utility that allows you to invoke queries, batch files, and commands. sqlcmd comes in two flavors: one that is integrated in SSMS and one that can be invoked from the command.

The one that is integrated from within SSMS can be toggled on or off from the **Query** menu item and the **SQLCMD Mode** option:

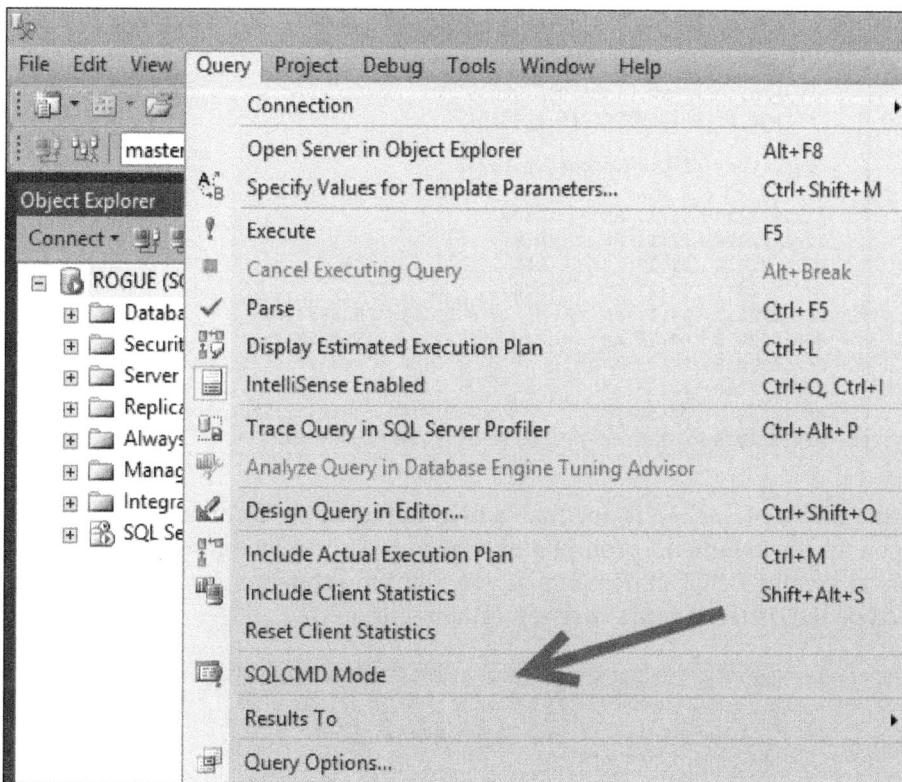

When toggled on, the **SQLCMD Mode** menu allows for a limited set of the sqlcmd commands to be entered and invoked from **SSMS Query Editor**.

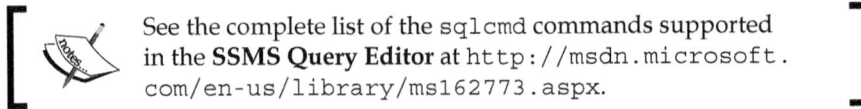

> See the complete list of the sqlcmd commands supported in the **SSMS Query Editor** at http://msdn.microsoft.com/en-us/library/ms162773.aspx.

For example, !! allows you to execute any operating system commands. You will also notice that once the command is recognized, the whole line becomes shaded in gray:

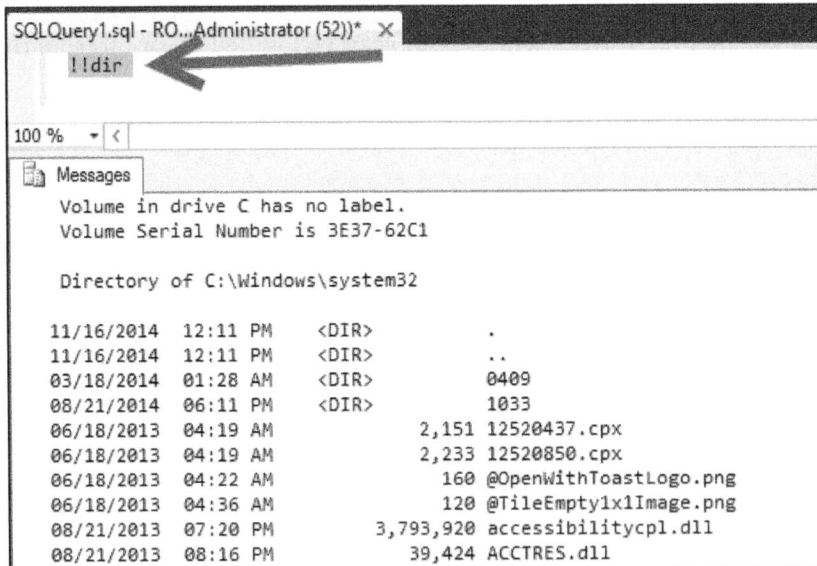

```
SQLQuery1.sql - RO...Administrator (52))*  ✕

    !!dir

100 %  ▾ ‹

  Messages
    Volume in drive C has no label.
    Volume Serial Number is 3E37-62C1

    Directory of C:\Windows\system32

    11/16/2014  12:11 PM  <DIR>          .
    11/16/2014  12:11 PM  <DIR>          ..
    03/18/2014  01:28 AM  <DIR>          0409
    08/21/2014  06:11 PM  <DIR>          1033
    06/18/2013  04:19 AM          2,151 12520437.cpx
    06/18/2013  04:19 AM          2,233 12520850.cpx
    06/18/2013  04:22 AM            160 @OpenWithToastLogo.png
    06/18/2013  04:36 AM            120 @TileEmpty1x1Image.png
    08/21/2013  07:20 PM      3,793,920 accessibilitycpl.dll
    08/21/2013  08:16 PM         39,424 ACCTRES.dll
```

The other flavor of sqlcmd is one that is invoked from the command prompt. You can open up the command prompt and type in sqlcmd. Once connected, you can execute any valid T-SQL statements. If you want the statements to be executed right away, type the GO terminator after each statement:

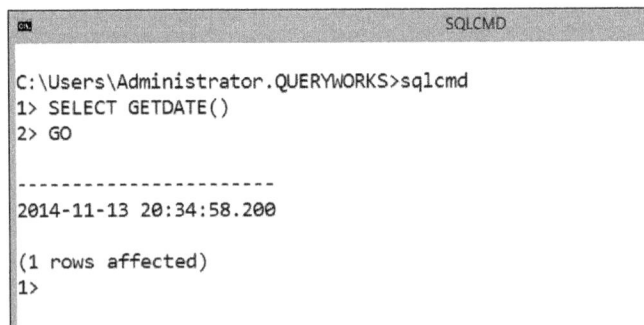

```
                                    SQLCMD

C:\Users\Administrator.QUERYWORKS>sqlcmd
1> SELECT GETDATE()
2> GO

------------------------
2014-11-13 20:34:58.200

(1 rows affected)
1>
```

In the example shown in the preceding screenshot, since we haven't provided any parameters, the connection uses some default values. Invoking `sqlcmd` without parameters will attempt to connect to the default SQL Server instance using your Windows credentials. Your connection will be successful if you indeed have a default instance and if your Windows credential is mapped to a login in the default instance. Otherwise, you will receive an error message and will have to provide the correct values for the parameters.

These are the parameters available for `sqlcmd`, which you can get by executing the command `sqlcmd /?` in the **Command Prompt** window:

```
C:\Users\Administrator.QUERYWORKS>sqlcmd /?
Microsoft (R) SQL Server Command Line Tool
Version 12.0.2000.8 NT
Copyright (c) 2014 Microsoft. All rights reserved.

usage: Sqlcmd            [-U login id]          [-P password]
  [-S server]            [-H hostname]          [-E trusted connection]
  [-N Encrypt Connection][-C Trust Server Certificate]
  [-d use database name] [-l login timeout]     [-t query timeout]
  [-h headers]           [-s colseparator]      [-w screen width]
  [-a packetsize]        [-e echo input]        [-I Enable Quoted Identifiers]
  [-c cmdend]            [-L[c] list servers[clean output]]
  [-q "cmdline query"]   [-Q "cmdline query" and exit]
  [-m errorlevel]        [-V severitylevel]     [-W remove trailing spaces]
  [-u unicode output]    [-r[0|1] msgs to stderr]
  [-i inputfile]         [-o outputfile]        [-z new password]
  [-f <codepage> | i:<codepage>[,o:<codepage>]] [-Z new password and exit]
  [-k[1|2] remove[replace] control characters]
  [-y variable length type display width]
  [-Y fixed length type display width]
  [-p[1] print statistics[colon format]]
  [-R use client regional setting]
  [-K application intent]
  [-M multisubnet failover]
  [-b On error batch abort]
  [-v var = "value"...]  [-A dedicated admin connection]
  [-X[1] disable commands, startup script, environment variables [and exit]]
  [-x disable variable substitution]
  [-? show syntax summary]
```

A lot of the parameters listed in the full `sqlcmd` help result shown in the preceding screenshot are the same parameters you will see in the `Invoke-Sqlcmd` cmdlet:

```
Invoke-Sqlcmd

[[-Query] <String>]

[-AbortOnError]

[-ConnectionTimeout <Int32>]
```

```
[-Database <String>]
[-DedicatedAdministratorConnection]
[-DisableCommands]
[-DisableVariables]
[-EncryptConnection]
[-ErrorLevel <Int32>]
[-HostName <String>]
[-IgnoreProviderContext]
[-IncludeSqlUserErrors]
[-InputFile <String>]
[-MaxBinaryLength <Int32>]
[-MaxCharLength <Int32>]
[-NewPassword <String>]
[-OutputSqlErrors <Boolean>]
[-Password <String>]
[-QueryTimeout <Int32>]
[-ServerInstance <PSObject>]
[-SeverityLevel <Int32>]
[-SuppressProviderContextWarning]
[-Username <String>]
[-Variable <String[]>]
[<CommonParameters>]
```

Sending a really simple query to the server will take a format similar to the following command:

```
Invoke-Sqlcmd -ServerInstance $servername -Database $database -Query
$query
```

Most of the time, you will have to specify the server and database you are connecting to, along with your credentials. The parameters you specify will vary depending on your requirements and configurations. But overall, it's a fairly straightforward command.

If you encounter issues running Invoke-SqlCmd, with errors indicating that it's not recognized, this could be the result of processor version incompatibility. You can try running the 32-bit PowerShell console or ISE to see if this resolves the issue. The other alternative is explicitly installing the PSProvider DLLs, as described at http://www.systemcentercentral.com/fix-invoke-sqlcmd-is-not-recognized-in-powershell-on-windows-8-1-and-2012/.

There have been some issues reported with the QueryTimeout parameter of Invoke-Sqlcmd. The QueryTimeout value is in seconds and needs to be between 1 and 65535. In SQL Server 2008 and earlier, it has been reported that the QueryTimeout of 0 (which should mean no timeout) is not honored. Check out the Microsoft Connect item at https://connect.microsoft.com/SQLServer/feedback/details/551799/invoke-sqlcmd-querytimeout-0-still-times-out. There are some workarounds, including a function called Invoke-Sqlcmd2 provided by Chad Miller, which is also posted in the Microsoft Connect item.

ADO.NET

It is possible to use ADO.NET within PowerShell to pass queries and commands to SQL Server. If you have done some ADO.NET with C# or VB.NET, then the code will look similar, except for the fact that it's in PowerShell.

When using ADO.NET, you are required to use the System.Data.SqlClient class. Here is an example of how you would connect to SQL Server and retrieve records from a table:

```
$conn = New-Object System.Data.SqlClient.SqlConnection
$conn.ConnectionString = "Server=ROGUE;Database=Chinook;
  Integrated Security=True"
$cmd = New-Object System.Data.SqlClient.SqlCommand
$cmd.CommandText = "SELECT * FROM Album"
$cmd.Connection = $conn
$adapter = New-Object System.Data.SqlClient.SqlDataAdapter
$adapter.SelectCommand = $cmd
$dataset = New-Object System.Data.DataSet
$adapter.Fill($dataset)
$conn.Close()
$dataset.Tables[0]
```

The preceding example uses the SqlDataAdapter class to issue the command and the DataSet class to capture the results.

An overview of the features, security, and behavior of SQL Server and ADO.NET is provided at `http://msdn.microsoft.com/en-us/library/kb9s9ks0(v=vs.110).aspx`. To learn more about populating an ADO.NET `DataSet` from a `DataAdapter`, visit `http://msdn.microsoft.com/en-us/library/bh8kx08z(v=vs.110).aspx`.

Using straight up ADO.NET may not be the ideal way to send your queries, since your script will end up being more code-heavy than it needs to be. If it is doable with `Invoke-Sqlcmd`, it may be simpler to use this cmdlet to send your queries. We will see a number of examples regarding the same later in this chapter.

The Invoke-Expression cmdlet

Yet another alternative to sending queries and commands to SQL Server is the `Invoke-Expression` cmdlet. The `Invoke-Expression` cmdlet syntax is pretty short. It just requires the command and the parameters:

`Invoke-Expression [-Command] <String> [ <CommonParameters>]` If you are invoking an executable—for example, the SQL Server `bcp` utility—the `Invoke-Expression` cmdlet can be utilized. A short snippet looks like the following command:

```
Invoke-Expression $bcp
```

In the preceding command, we assume `$bcp` contains the full command and options we require when running the `bcp` (bulk copy) utility. We will discuss this in more detail later in the chapter.

Sending simple queries to SQL Server – different variations

To send simple queries to SQL Server, you can use the `Invoke-Sqlcmd` cmdlet with the instance name, database name, and query. The query can be wrapped in a here-string parameter to make it easier to read and edit.

The following is an example that passes a simple SELECT statement to SQL Server using the current Windows context:

```
Import-Module SQLPS -DisableNameChecking

$servername = "ROGUE"    # or localhost
```

```
$database = "Chinook"

#query inside a here-string
$query = @"
SELECT
    TOP 10 *
FROM
    dbo.Album
"@

#if not providing username and password
#then uses current context
Invoke-Sqlcmd -ServerInstance $servername -Database
  $database -Query $query | Format-Table
```

The results will be displayed on the PowerShell console as shown in the following screenshot:

```
AlbumId Title                                                      ArtistId
------- -----                                                      --------
      1 For Those About To Rock We Sal...                                 1
      2 Balls to the Wall                                                 2
      3 Restless and Wild                                                 2
      4 Let There Be Rock                                                 1
      5 Big Ones                                                          3
      6 Jagged Little Pill                                                4
      7 Facelift                                                          5
      8 Warner 25 Anos                                                    6
      9 Plays Metallica By Four Cellos                                    7
     10 Audioslave                                                        8
```

If you need to use a SQL login, you should supply values to the Username and Password parameters as well. If you want to capture the results in a file, you can pipe the command to an Out-File cmdlet:

```
Invoke-Sqlcmd -ServerInstance $servername -Database
  $database -Query $query | Out-File "C:\Temp\results.rpt"
```

Piping the command to the Out-File cmdlet simply captures the results that were supposed to be displayed onscreen into the file. However, if you want the results captured in a formatted format—for example, a **comma separated value (CSV)**—you can use an export cmdlet such as Export-Csv:

```
Invoke-Sqlcmd -ServerInstance $servername -Database $database
  -Query $query | Export-Csv -NoTypeInformation
  -Path "C:\Temp\results.csv"
```

We have to specify `-NoTypeInformation` so that the first line of the CSV file does not contain metadata about the results. You don't have to hardcode the query in your script. `Invoke-Sqlcmd` can get the query from a file as long as it's properly identified in the `InputFile` parameter:

```
Invoke-Sqlcmd -ServerInstance $servername -Database $database -InputFile
$file
```

The `sqlcmd` utility supports variables and values can be passed into the query or the file when `sqlcmd` is invoked. This capability is also supported in the `Invoke-Sqlcmd` cmdlet.

For example, if the input file contains the following script:

```
SELECT *
FROM Album
WHERE AlbumId = $(AlbumId)
```

In the preceding script, `$(AlbumId)` is a variable and the value can be replaced on execution time. To do this in PowerShell, you have to list the variable and its value and pass it to `Invoke-Sqlcmd` using the `-Variable` parameter:

```
$variables = "AlbumId = 2"
Invoke-Sqlcmd -ServerInstance $servername -Database
  $database -InputFile $file -Variable $variables
```

PowerShell really shines when we can start stitching multiple cmdlets together—in this case, both SQL Server-specific and non-SQL Server-specific cmdlets. For example, we can have a list of servers in a text file. With PowerShell, it is fairly easy to read the contents of this text file using the `Get-Content` cmdlet. We can then iterate through this list using the `ForEach-Object` cmdlet and execute a query (or multiple queries) to each of the instances.

Here is a simple example that illustrates sending a query to multiple servers:

```
#get a list of instances from a file
$file = "C:\Temp\servers.txt"


#execute query to multiple instances
Get-Content $file |
ForEach-Object {
   Invoke-Sqlcmd -ServerInstance $_ -Database $database
   -Query $query
}
```

What if you want to not just display results, but also capture the results so you can work with the returned rows? With PowerShell, you can store the results in a variable:

```
$variables = "AlbumId = 2"
$results = Invoke-Sqlcmd -ServerInstance $servername -Database $database
-InputFile $file -Variable $variables
```

If we pipe this variable to `Get-Member`, we will discover that the data type it takes on is `System.Data.DataRow`. The same is displayed in the following screenshot:

```
PS SQLSERVER:\> $results | Get-Member


    TypeName: System.Data.DataRow

Name            MemberType          Definition
----            ----------          ----------
AcceptChanges   Method              void AcceptChanges()
BeginEdit       Method              void BeginEdit()
CancelEdit      Method              void CancelEdit()
ClearErrors     Method              void ClearErrors()
Delete          Method              void Delete()
EndEdit         Method              void EndEdit()
```

What we will also see, as we scroll down the list of properties, is that the columns of the result set are converted into properties. In the following screenshot, you will see `AlbumId`, `ArtistId`, and `Title` as properties:

```
SetParentRow    Method                   void SetParentRow(System.Dat
ToString        Method                   string ToString()
Item            ParameterizedProperty    System.Object Item(int colum
AlbumId         Property                 int AlbumId {get;set;}
ArtistId        Property                 int ArtistId {get;set;}
Title           Property                 string Title {get;set;}
```

This is good news, because this tells us we can easily access the columns by treating them as properties. To work on each record in the result set, you can pipe the results variable into a `ForEach-Object` cmdlet. Here is a starter snippet you can use:

```
$results |
ForEach-Object {
    #get current row
    $row = $_

    #get the title
```

```
    $row.Title


    #your other code here
}
```

Fixing orphaned users

In *Chapter 4, Basic SQL Server Administration*, we talked about how we can list orphaned users in SQL Server. An orphaned user is a database user that is no longer mapped to a valid instance login. Using SMO, you may be tempted to do something like the following snippet:

```
#unfortunately this doesn't work
$user.Login = "JDoe";
$user.Alter();
$user.Refresh();
```

In the preceding script, we are simply assigning a new login to an SMO database user object and invoking the Alter() method. Syntactically and logically, this should work. However, it doesn't. In this case, we will need to resort to sending an actual ALTER T-SQL command to SQL Server to fix an orphaned user. The snippet that can accomplish this task is as follows:

```
$username = "kurapika"
$query = @"
  ALTER USER $($username)
  WITH LOGIN = $($login)
"@
Invoke-Sqlcmd -ServerInstance $server -Database
  $database -Query $query
```

Once this code finishes executing, you can verify that the database user has indeed been mapped to the login you specified.

Getting fragmentation data

In a previous chapter, we listed fragmentation information using the EnumFragmentation() method. Using the EnumFragmentation() method can be quite slow. An alternative to using this method is using the **Dynamic Management Views (DMVs)** and the **Dynamic Management Functions (DMFs)** related to fragmentation. The following is an example of using the DMF dm_db_index_physical_stats() to query the average fragmentation for all indexes in a database:

```
Import-Module SQLPS -DisableNameChecking


#current server name
$servername = "ROGUE"
$database = "Chinook"


$query = @"
SELECT
  OBJECT_NAME(phys_stats.OBJECT_ID) AS [Object],
  idx.name AS [Index Name],
  phys_stats.index_type_desc [Index Type],
  phys_stats.avg_fragmentation_in_percent [Fragmentation %],
  phys_stats.page_count [# Pages]
FROM
  sys.dm_db_index_physical_stats(DB_ID(),NULL, NULL, NULL ,
    N'LIMITED') AS phys_stats
  INNER JOIN sys.indexes AS idx WITH (NOLOCK)
  ON phys_stats.[object_id] = idx.[object_id]
  AND phys_stats.index_id = idx.index_id
WHERE
  phys_stats.database_id = DB_ID()
ORDER BY
  phys_stats.avg_fragmentation_in_percent DESC;
"@


Invoke-Sqlcmd -ServerInstance $servername -Database $database
  -Query $query | Format-Table -AutoSize
```

A sample result provides the object name, index name, type, fragmentation percentage, and number of index pages:

```
Object          Index Name                Index Type              Fragmentation %  # Pages
------          ----------                ----------              ---------------  -------
PlaylistTrack   IFK_PlaylistTrackTrackId  NONCLUSTERED INDEX               96.875       32
Track           IFK_TrackGenreId          NONCLUSTERED INDEX  90.9090909090909         11
Track           IFK_TrackAlbumId          NONCLUSTERED INDEX  88.8888888888889          9
Track           IFK_TrackMediaTypeId      NONCLUSTERED INDEX  85.7142857142857          7
PlaylistTrack   PK_PlaylistTrack          NONCLUSTERED INDEX  85.3658536585366         41
InvoiceLine     IFK_InvoiceLineTrackId    NONCLUSTERED INDEX                   80        5
InvoiceLine     IFK_InvoiceLineInvoiceId  NONCLUSTERED INDEX                   75        4
PlaylistTrack                             HEAP                                 50       20
Artist          PK_Artist                 CLUSTERED INDEX                      50        2
Customer        PK_Customer               CLUSTERED INDEX                      50        2
Album           PK_Album                  CLUSTERED INDEX     33.3333333333333          3
InvoiceLine     PK_InvoiceLine            CLUSTERED INDEX                      30       10
Invoice         PK_Invoice                CLUSTERED INDEX     14.2857142857143          7
```

When managing your databases, it's important to know these metrics so that you can selectively pick indexes that need to be reorganized, rebuilt, or left alone. As a rule of thumb, you want to reorganize indexes with at least 10 to 30 percent age fragmentation and at least a certain number of pages. You can start with at least 1000 pages, and, as you monitor your environment, you may vary this number.

Backing up and restoring databases

Even backup and restore can be done through `Invoke-Sqlcmd`. It is just a matter of passing the actual `BACKUP` and `RESTORE` command to `Invoke-Sqlcmd`. The following is an example:

```
Import-Module SQLPS -DisableNameChecking

#current server name
$servername = "ROGUE"      # or localhost
$database = "Chinook"

$query = @"
BACKUP DATABASE Chinook
TO DISK='Z:\Backups\Chinook.bak'
WITH
    FORMAT,
    COMPRESSION
"@
```

```
#code below in one line
Invoke-Sqlcmd -ServerInstance $servername -Database $database
  -Query $query
```

Although this is possible, it would be more elegant to use the `Backup-SqlDatabase` and `Restore-SqlDatabase` cmdlets (which were discussed in *Chapter 4*, *Basic SQL Server Administration*) since these are already provided with the SQLPS module.

Exporting data using bcp

SQL Server has a number of command prompt utilities that assist with database operations. All of these can be invoked from PowerShell using the `Invoke-Expression` cmdlet.

`bcp` is a well-known utility that allows for the fast import and export of data. The data transfer can be fairly straightforward; for example, if taking all the records from a table to a CSV file. It could also be more complex, which will require supplying a format file to specify the structure of the data. If we wanted to export all the records from the `Album` table in the `Chinook` database using a trusted connection with character data type, the `bcp` command will look like the following:

```
bcp Chinook.dbo.Album out C:\Temp\results.txt -T -c
```

To do this within PowerShell, we can compose the same command expression and pass it to `Invoke-Expression`:

```
$database = "Chinook"
$schema = "dbo"
$table = "Album"
$filename = "C:\Temp\results.txt"


$bcp = "bcp $($database).$($schema).$($table) out $filename -T -c"
Invoke-Expression $bcp
```

Once invoked, the following is the result you will see, which is typical of what you would see from a `bcp` operation:

```
Starting copy...

347 rows copied.
Network packet size (bytes): 4096
Clock Time (ms.) Total     : 1          Average : (347000.00 rows per sec.)
PS SQLSERVER:\>
```

Summary

In this chapter, we looked at different ways of sending queries and commands to SQL Server using PowerShell. We saw that, in addition to using the cmdlets `Invoke-Sqlcmd` and `Invoke-Expression`, we can also utilize ADO.NET and SMO. We also learned to that although in most cases we can use PowerShell to query SQL Server, we have to consider if there are better tools to assist us in accomplishing our task.

In the next chapter, we will look at tasks that help monitor and automate SQL Server, and see how these are accomplished using PowerShell.

6
Monitoring and Automating SQL Server

This chapter covers how SQL Server usage and performance monitoring, logging, alerting, and error checking can be done with PowerShell. The topics covered in this chapter include the following:

- Getting to know helpful cmdlets
- Scheduling PowerShell scripts
- Checking logs
- Monitoring failed jobs
- Alerting on disk space usage
- Logging blocked processes
- Getting performance metrics

Getting to know helpful cmdlets

Before we start covering any SQL Server-specific snippets, it's good to identify cmdlets that are frequently used when you are monitoring and logging any activities. The cmdlets described in this section are the ones you will (most likely) frequently use. Remember to use Get-Help to get the full documentation on syntax, parameter sets, and examples.

The Send-MailMessage cmdlet

Simply stated, the `Send-MailMessage` cmdlet allows you to e-mail something from PowerShell, which is a pretty useful action when you are monitoring something and want to get some alerts or reports via e-mail. This is the syntax of `Send-MailMessage` from TechNet:

```
Send-MailMessage [-To] <String[]> [-Subject] <String>
  [[-Body] <String> ] [[-SmtpServer] <String> ] -From <String>
  [-Attachments <String[]> ] [-Bcc <String[]> ] [-BodyAsHtml]
  [-Cc <String[]> ] [-Credential <PSCredential> ]
  [-DeliveryNotificationOption <DeliveryNotificationOptions> ]
  [-Encoding <Encoding> ] [-Port <Int32> ]
  [-Priority <MailPriority> ] [-UseSsl] [ <CommonParameters>]
```

The ConvertTo-Html cmdlet

When sending e-mail messages, you may want some messages to be formatted in HTML. This will come in handy when you are e-mailing tables of values within the e-mail body. Here is one of the parameter sets for `ConvertTo-Html` from TechNet:

```
ConvertTo-Html [[-Property] <Object[]> ] [[-Head] <String[]> ]
  [[-Title] <String> ] [[-Body] <String[]> ] [-As <String> ]
  [-CssUri <Uri> ] [-InputObject <PSObject> ]
  [-PostContent <String[]> ] [-PreContent <String[]> ]
  [ <CommonParameters>]
```

The Export-Csv cmdlet

Alternatively, you may want to store some reports in a CSV file and, later on, either open it in a spreadsheet or import it into a database. When that's the case, the `Export-Csv` cmdlet is your friend. It converts your results into **comma separated value (CSV)** strings and stores them in a file. The following is the syntax of `Export-Csv` from TechNet:

```
Export-Csv [[-Path] <String> ] [[-Delimiter] <Char> ]
  -InputObject <PSObject> [-Append] [-Encoding <String> ] [-Force]
  [-LiteralPath <String> ] [-NoClobber] [-NoTypeInformation]
  [-Confirm] [-WhatIf] [ <CommonParameters>]
```

The Write-EventLog cmdlet

If, instead of exporting to a file or sending an e-mail out, you want all the alerts in your event log, PowerShell offers a cmdlet that allows you to do so. The `Write-EventLog` cmdlet allows you to insert an entry into an existing event log on your system. The source, however, must have been registered already for the event log. The following is the syntax of `Write-EventLog` from TechNet:

```
Write-EventLog [-LogName] <String> [-Source] <String> [-EventId]
  <Int32> [[-EntryType] <EventLogEntryType> ] [-Message] <String>
  [-Category <Int16> ] [-ComputerName <String> ] [-RawData <Byte[]> ]
  [ <CommonParameters>]
```

Additional cmdlets

There are a number of other cmdlets that can be used to log or store any information you collect while monitoring SQL Server. Explore `Out-File` and `Add-Content` for saving data to a file. You can also use `Invoke-SqlCmd`, especially if you're going to be storing information in SQL Server tables or sending queries over to your database.

Scheduling PowerShell scripts

Many of the examples covered in this chapter can be run ad hoc. However, to enable more continuous monitoring, you will need to schedule these scripts to run regularly. You can use a number of options for scheduling. You can take advantage of SQL Server Agent and you can create a job that uses either a **PowerShell** step or an **Operating System (CmdExec)** step. Alternatively, you can use Windows Task Scheduler or vendor-specific schedulers, if they are available to you.

Checking logs

We can use SQL **Server Management Objects (SMO)** to check the SQL Server error log. The script that picks out anything in the logs that have the words *failed* or *error* looks like the following:

```
$content = ($server.ReadErrorLog() |
Where-Object {$_.Text -like "*failed*" -or $_.Text -like "*error*"})
```

We can wrap this in code that allows us to send these entries to our DBA (or DBA team) via e-mail. Sending e-mail in PowerShell can be done using the cmdlet `Send-MailMessage`. `Send-MailMessage` will accept sender and recipient e-mail addresses, mail server information, subject, content, and, optionally, attachments. The content can either be in text or HTML format. If you are sending an HTML e-mail, you can convert the message into HTML by using `ConvertTo-Html`. Optionally, you can specify an external CSS with `ConvertTo-Html` using the `-CssUri` parameter.

The full script that picks out and e-mails the last 10 entries using a Windows authenticated local account is as follows:

```
Import-Module SQLPS -DisableNameChecking


#current server name
$servername = "ROGUE"    # or localhost


$server = New-Object "Microsoft.SqlServer.Management.Smo.
  Server" $servername


#get the last 10 error entries, and convert to HTML
$content = ($server.ReadErrorLog() |
Where-Object {$_.Text -like "*failed*" -or $_.Text -like "*error*"
  -or $_.HasErrors -eq $true} |
Select-Object LogDate, ProcessInfo, Text, HasErrors  -Last 10   |
ConvertTo-Html)


#email settings
$currdate = Get-Date -Format "yyyy-MM-dd hmmtt"
$smtp = "mail.rogue.local"
$to = "DBA <administrator@rogue.local>"
$from = "DBMail <dbmail@administrator.local>"
$subject = "Last 10 Errors as of $currdate"


#send the email
Send-MailMessage -SmtpServer $smtp -To $to -from $from  -Subject
  $subject -Body "$($content)" -BodyAsHtml
```

What you should expect in your mailbox is an e-mail that looks like the following one:

LogDate	ProcessInfo	Text
Last 10 Errors as of 2014-11-28 117PM		
From DBMail to DBA		
11/28/2014 10:22:12 AM	Server	Logging SQL Server messages in file 'C:\Program Files\Microsoft SQL Server\MSSQL12.MSSQLSERVER\MSSQL\Log\ERRORLOG'.
11/28/2014 10:22:12 AM	Server	Registry startup parameters: -d C:\Program Files\Microsoft SQL Server\MSSQL12.MSSQLSERVER\MSSQL\DATA\master.mdf -e C:\Program Files\M Server\MSSQL12.MSSQLSERVER\MSSQL\Log\ERRORLOG -l C:\Program Files\Micro Server\MSSQL12.MSSQLSERVER\MSSQL\DATA\mastlog.ldf
11/28/2014 1:09:13 PM	Logon	Error: 18456, Severity: 14, State: 58.
11/28/2014 1:09:13 PM	Logon	Login failed for user 'dsdssds'. Reason: An attempt to login using SQL authenticati Windows authentication only. [CLIENT: <local machine>]
11/28/2014 1:09:22 PM	Logon	Error: 18456, Severity: 14, State: 58.
11/28/2014 1:09:22 PM	Logon	Login failed for user 'someonetryingtohack'. Reason: An attempt to login using SQ configured for Windows authentication only. [CLIENT: <local machine>]
11/28/2014 1:09:27 PM	Logon	Error: 18456, Severity: 14, State: 58.
11/28/2014 1:09:27 PM	Logon	Login failed for user 'letmein'. Reason: An attempt to login using SQL authenticatio Windows authentication only. [CLIENT: <local machine>]
11/28/2014 1:09:32 PM	Logon	Error: 18456, Severity: 14, State: 58.
11/28/2014 1:09:32 PM	Logon	Login failed for user 'whoareyou'. Reason: An attempt to login using SQL authentic Windows authentication only. [CLIENT: <local machine>]

If you want to use a mail server such as Gmail, you will need to adjust your server and port settings. Most other providers will also use **Secure Socket Layer** (SSL). Instead of hardcoding the credentials, you should also prompt for the credentials using the `Get-Credential` cmdlet. Here is a sample snippet, with the pertinent code highlighted:

```
#email settings
$currdate = Get-Date -Format "yyyy-MM-dd hhmmtt"
$smtp = "smtp.gmail.com"
$port = "587"
$to = "recipient@YourDomain.com"
$from = "sender@gmail.com"
$subject = "Last 10 Errors as of $currdate"
```

```
$attachment = "C:\path\to\attachment.txt"


#send the email
#code below should be in a single line
Send-MailMessage -SmtpServer $smtp -port $port -UseSSl -Credential
  (Get-Credential) -To $to -from $from  -Subject $subject -Body
  "$($content)" -BodyAsHtml -Attachments $attachment
```

Monitoring failed jobs

We can monitor and be alerted on failed jobs as well. This is the basic snippet that gets this information:

```
$server.JobServer.Jobs |

Where-Object LastRunOutcome -eq "Failed"
```

In the following sample, we are listing all failed jobs and sending an e-mail report out:

```
Import-Module SQLPS -DisableNameChecking


#current server name
$servername = "ROGUE"
$server = New-Object "Microsoft.SqlServer.Management.Smo.
  Server" $servername


#get a list of jobs that failed, and convert to HTML
$content = ($server.JobServer.Jobs |
Where-Object LastRunOutcome -eq "Failed" |
Select-Object Name, LastRunDate |
ConvertTo-Html)


#email settings
$currdate = Get-Date -Format "yyyy-MM-dd hmmtt"
$smtp = "mail.rogue.local"
$to = "DBA <administrator@rogue.local>"
$from = "DBMail <dbmail@administrator.local>"
$subject = "Failed Jobs as of $currdate"

    Send-MailMessage -SmtpServer $smtp -To $to -from $from  -Subject
      $subject -Body "$($content)" -BodyAsHtml
```

The e-mail that gets sent out will look like the following:

```
Failed Jobs as of 2014-11-28 101PM

          From DBMail
          to DBA


                  Name                          LastRunDate
Export Client Data                        10/23/2014 12:34:39 PM
ROGUE-Registration-1                      11/28/2014 9:02:39 AM
ROGUE-Registration-Registration-ROGUE\SQL2014-3 11/28/2014 9:02:39 AM
Test Job                                  11/28/2014 10:24:25 AM
```

Alerting on disk space usage

In this example, we will do something a little bit different from the first two snippets. Here, we are going to report on disk usage. The basic snippet that gets this information is as follows:

```
Get-WmiObject -Class Win32_LogicalDisk -ComputerName $servername
```

If you want to report on only physical drives, you can add the following filter:

```
Where-Object DriveType -eq 3
```

In the e-mail we send out, however, we will add a little bit more formatting. We can do this by providing an inline CSS in the table we are constructing. In addition to general formatting, we are also creating a CSS class that we will assign to a row when that row's free disk space falls below a critical threshold that we assign.

The script is provided here. The script is a little bit long because of the **HyperText Markup Language (HTML)** and **Cascading Style Sheet (CSS)** construction. But some inline comments have been provided to explain the code:

```
#current server name
$servername = "ROGUE"


#if free space % falls below this threshold,
#assign CSS class "critical" which makes font red
$criticalthreshold = 10


#inline css for styling
```

```
$inlinecss = @"
<style>
   table
   {
       margin: 0px;
       border: 1px solid #7e7e7e;
       background-color: #fafafa;
       border-collapse: collapse;
   }

   #every other row has different color
   tr:nth-child(even) /* doesnt work in IE8 */
   {
       background-color: #d5e4f4;
   }

   th, td
   {
       width: 100px;
       text-align: left;
   }

   th
   {
       background-color:#a6bdd6;
       font-weight:bold;
   }

   #anything marked as critical is styled bold and red
   .critical, .critical td
   {
       color: red;
       font-weight: bold;
   }
</style>
"@

#construct the html content
$htmlhead = "<head><title>Disk Space Report </title>$($inlinecss)</head>"
$htmlbody = "<body>"
```

```
$htmlbody += "<p>$($subject)</p>"

#below creates table headers
$htmlbody += "<table><tbody>"
$htmlbody += "<th>Device ID</th>"
$htmlbody += "<th>Size (GB)</th>"
$htmlbody += "<th>Free Space (GB)</th>"
$htmlbody += "<th>Free Space (%)</th>"

#table content is dynamically generated from Get-WmiObject
#here we extract disk usage
#to look only at Local Disk, add filter for DriveType -eq 3
Get-WmiObject -Class Win32_LogicalDisk -ComputerName $servername |
ForEach-Object {
    $disk = $_
    $size = "{0:N1}" -f ($disk.Size/1GB)
    $freespace = "{0:N1}" -f ($disk.FreeSpace/1GB)
    if ($disk.Size -gt 0)
    {
      $freespacepercent = "{0:P0}" -f ($disk.FreeSpace/$disk.Size)
    }
    else
    {
      $freespacepercent = ""
    }
    if ($freespacepercent -ne "" -and $freespacepercent -le
      $criticalthreshold)
    {
      $htmlbody += "<tr class='critical'>"
    }
    else
    {
      $htmlbody += "<tr>"
    }
    $htmlbody += "<td>$($disk.DeviceID)</td>"
    $htmlbody += "<td>$($size)</td>"
    $htmlbody += "<td>$($freespace)</td>"
    $htmlbody += "<td>$($freespacepercent)</td>"
    $htmlbody += "</tr>"
}
```

```
$htmlbody += "</tbody></table></body></html>"

#compose full html content
$htmlcontent = $htmlhead + $htmlbody

#email settings
$currdate = Get-Date -Format "yyyy-MM-dd hmmtt"
$smtp = "mail.rogue.local"
$to = "DBA <administrator@rogue.local>"
$from = "DBMail <dbmail@administrator.local>"
$subject = "Disk Space Report for $servername as of $currdate"

Send-MailMessage -SmtpServer $smtp -To $to -from $from  -Subject
  $subject -Body "$($htmlcontent)" -BodyAsHtml
```

The result looks like the following screenshot. Notice in the following sample that D drive's free space percentage falls below the threshold we set (which was 10), which is why the entry is in bold and in red:

Disk Space Report for ROGUE as of 2014-11-29 602AM

From DBMail
to DBA

Disk Space Report for ROGUE as of 2014-11-29 602AM

Device ID	Size (GB)	Free Space (GB)	Free Space (%)
A:	0.0	0.0	
C:	120.0	98.7	82 %
D:	2.4	0.0	0 %

Logging blocked processes

In this example, we are going to see log blocking processes in the Windows Event Log. You will need to ensure that you are running this script with elevated privileges, that is, as administrator. This is the snippet to check for blocking processes:

```
$server.EnumProcesses() |
Where-Object IsSystem -eq $false |
Where-Object BlockingSpid -gt 0
```

To log using a custom source, you can add the following block to check if the source name exists, and, if not, create it:

```
#check if Event Log source exists, otherwise create
if(!([System.Diagnostics.EventLog]::SourceExists($source)))
{
    New-EventLog -LogName $logname -Source $source
}
```

The cmdlet that writes to the event log is `Write-EventLog`, and it requires the log name, source, event type, event ID, entry type, and message. The following is the whole script:

```
Import-Module SQLPS -DisableNameChecking


$logname = "Application"
$source = "SQL Server Custom"


#current server name
$servername = "ROGUE"


$server = New-Object "Microsoft.SqlServer.Management.Smo.
  Server" $servername


$blockedprocesses = $server.EnumProcesses() |
Where-Object IsSystem -eq $false |
Where-Object BlockingSpid -gt 0 |
Select-Object Spid, Database, BlockingSpid,
Login, Status


#check if Event Log source exists, otherwise create
if(!([System.Diagnostics.EventLog]::SourceExists($source)))
{
    Write-Output "Creating a new source"
    New-EventLog -LogName $logname -Source $source
}


#compose message
```

```
$message = "Blocked Process Identified `r`n`r`n" + $blockedprocesses


#write to event log with custom source
Write-EventLog -LogName $logname -Source $source -EventId 1
  -EntryType Warning -Message $message
```

Once this script runs, and if there are any blocked processes, you should find a **Warning** entry in your **Windows Event Viewer** about a blocked process (as shown in the following screenshot):

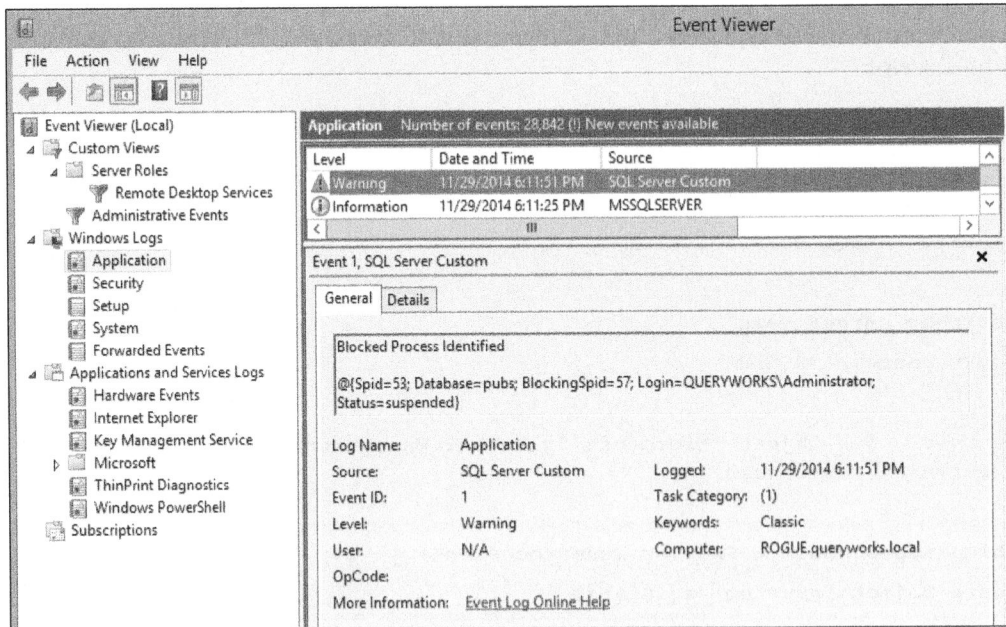

Getting performance metrics

We can also programmatically create **Data Collector Sets** in **Performance Monitor** and choose to start, run, and/or schedule them in PowerShell. We can list all the counter sets by running the following script, which uses the SMO server object:

```
#current server name
$servername = "ROGUE"     # or localhost


Get-Counter -ComputerName $servername -ListSet * |
Sort-Object CounterSetName |
Select-Object CounterSetName |
Format-Table
```

This will be a long list of counter sets. But some of the typical ones we usually look at are as follows:

- Memory
- Network Interface
- LogicalDisk
- PhysicalDisk
- Processor

When you go through the list, note that you will also find instance-specific counters. Here are some of the instance-specific counters I have in my system for my named instance SQL2014:

- MSSQL$SQL2014:Access Methods
- MSSQL$SQL2014:Availability Replica
- MSSQL$SQL2014:Backup Device
- MSSQL$SQL2014:Batch Resp Statistics
- MSSQL$SQL2014:Broker Activation
- MSSQL$SQL2014:Broker Statistics
- MSSQL$SQL2014:Broker TO Statistics
- MSSQL$SQL2014:Broker/DBM Transport
- MSSQL$SQL2014:Buffer Manager
- MSSQL$SQL2014:Buffer Node
- MSSQL$SQL2014:Catalog Metadata
- MSSQL$SQL2014:CLR
- MSSQL$SQL2014:Cursor Manager by Type
- MSSQL$SQL2014:Cursor Manager Total
- MSSQL$SQL2014:Database Mirroring
- MSSQL$SQL2014:Database Replica
- MSSQL$SQL2014:Databases
- MSSQL$SQL2014:Deprecated Features
- MSSQL$SQL2014:Exec Statistics
- MSSQL$SQL2014:FileTable
- MSSQL$SQL2014:General Statistics
- MSSQL$SQL2014:HTTP Storage
- MSSQL$SQL2014:Latches
- MSSQL$SQL2014:Locks

If you want to look at the actual counters in each counter set, you can use the `Get-Counter` cmdlet:

```
(Get-Counter -ListSet Memory).Counter
```

The following screenshot shows a partial view of what you should see:

```
\Memory\Page Faults/sec
\Memory\Available Bytes
\Memory\Committed Bytes
\Memory\Commit Limit
\Memory\Write Copies/sec
\Memory\Transition Faults/sec
\Memory\Cache Faults/sec
\Memory\Demand Zero Faults/sec
\Memory\Pages/sec
\Memory\Pages Input/sec
\Memory\Page Reads/sec
\Memory\Pages Output/sec
\Memory\Pool Paged Bytes
\Memory\Pool Nonpaged Bytes
\Memory\Page Writes/sec
\Memory\Pool Paged Allocs
\Memory\Pool Nonpaged Allocs
\Memory\Free System Page Table Entries
\Memory\Cache Bytes
\Memory\Cache Bytes Peak
\Memory\Pool Paged Resident Bytes
\Memory\System Code Total Bytes
\Memory\System Code Resident Bytes
\Memory\System Driver Total Bytes
\Memory\System Driver Resident Bytes
\Memory\System Cache Resident Bytes
```

At this point, you may be overwhelmed with the number of counters we just looked at. Indeed, there are a lot of counters. But when we are monitoring and troubleshooting our databases, it is best to know which counters to look at or focus on when troubleshooting specific issues.

Quest Software, now part of Dell, previously published a poster that identified the relevant counters for SQL Server, what they mean, and what you should look out for. At the time of writing of this book, this poster was still available for download. Just bring up your favorite search engine and look for `perfmon counters of interest` or `Quest perfmon poster`. Either search should yield a link to the PDF version of the post.

Just to give you an idea, this is what the poster looks like at a glance:

Each different section/block represents counters for specific areas. Three sections/blocks are mentioned for the sake of examples as follows:

- **Buffer & Memory Performance Counters**
- **Workload Performance Counters**
- **OS CPU & Processor Counters**

To create a **Data Collector Set** in PowerShell, we will have to use a **Performance Logs and Alerts (PLA)** DataCollectorSet object. You can read more about PLA from http://msdn.microsoft.com/en-us/library/windows/desktop/bb509354%28v=vs.85%29.aspx.

PLA `DataCollectorSets` have some enumerations that we will need to use when we are programmatically creating **Data Collector Sets**. We have to familiarize ourselves with the actual values before we can use them. Here are some of the available enumerations with partial screenshot-captures from their official TechNet documentation pages:

- **AutoPathFormat enumeration**: This enumeration is used for the subdirectory names/format, which allows you to specify in what format the generated subdirectory and filenames will be in. For example, `plaYearMonth` will give you a format like `201411` for November 2014. The hexadecimal values are the actual values of the enumeration, which we need to pass in our script:

AutoPathFormat enumeration

Defines how to decorate the file name or subdirectory name.

Syntax

C++

```
typedef enum  {
    plaNone                 = 0x0000,
    plaPattern              = 0x0001,
    plaComputer             = 0x0002,
    plaMonthDayHour         = 0x0100,
    plaSerialNumber         = 0x0200,
    plaYearDayOfYear        = 0x0400,
    plaYearMonth            = 0x0800,
    plaYearMonthDay         = 0x1000,
    plaYearMonthDayHour     = 0x2000,
    plaMonthDayHourMinute   = 0x4000
} AutoPathFormat;
```

- **FileFormat enumeration**: This enumeration allows you to choose the format of the file, whether it's text (tab delimited, comma separated, or SQL) or binary:

CommitMode enumeration

Defines the action to take when committing changes to the data collector set.

Syntax

```
C++

typedef enum  {
    plaCreateNew              = 0x0001,
    plaModify                 = 0x0002,
    plaCreateOrModify         = 0x0003,
    plaUpdateRunningInstance  = 0x0010,
    plaFlushTrace             = 0x0020,
    plaValidateOnly           = 0x1000
} CommitMode;
```

- **CommitMode enumeration**: This enumeration specifies what should happen when **Data Collector Set** is committed in the script. For example, `plaCreateOrModify` will create a new **Data Collector Set** if it doesn't exist, or modify an existing one if it already does:

FileFormat enumeration

Defines the format of the data in the log file.

Syntax

```
C++

typedef enum  {
    plaCommaSeparated  = 0,
    plaTabSeparated    = 1,
    plaSql             = 2,
    plaBinary          = 3
} FileFormat;
```

The script that creates **Data Collector Set** that captures a few key processor, memory, network, and physical disk counters is presented next. Note the comments included in the script that help describe what the different blocks do:

```
#current server name
$servername = "ROGUE"      # or localhost


#data collector set name
$dcsname = "SQL Performance Metrics"


$dcs = New-Object -COM Pla.DataCollectorSet
$dcs.DisplayName = $dcsname


#subdirectory format will have year and month
#enum value is plaYearMonth, which is 0x0800
$dcs.SubdirectoryFormat = 0x0800


#specify path where data collector set will be stored
#typically this will be in the system drive
$dcs.RootPath = "%systemdrive%\PerfLogs\Admin\" + $dcsname


#now need to set up each file
$datacollector = $dcs.DataCollectors.CreateDataCollector(0)


#file format is binary
#enum is plaBinary = 3
$datacollector.LogFileFormat = 3


$datacollector.FileName = $dcsname + "_"


#filename format will have year, month and day
#enum value is plaYearMonthDay 0x1000
$datacollector.FileNameFormat = 0x1000
$datacollector.SampleInterval = 15
$datacollector.LogAppend = $true


#these are the counters we want to capture
#you can add more to this, or can pull this from a file
$counters = @(
    "\Memory\Available MBytes",
```

```
    "\Network Interface(*)\Bytes Received/sec",
    "\Network Interface(*)\Bytes Sent/sec",
    "\PhysicalDisk\Avg. Disk Sec/Read",
    "\PhysicalDisk\Avg. Disk Sec/Write",
    "\PhysicalDisk\Avg. Disk Queue Length",
    "\Processor(_Total)\% Processor Time"
)

#add the counters to the data collector
$datacollector.PerformanceCounters = $counters
$dcs.DataCollectors.Add($datacollector)

#save datacollectorset
#name, server, commit mode, createnewormodify
$dcs.Commit("$dcsname" , $servername , 0x0003)
```

Once you run the script and start **Data Collector Set**, you can open up **Performance Monitor**. One way is to type perfmon in your Windows search. You should see a new entry under the **User Defined** node under **Data Collector Sets**:

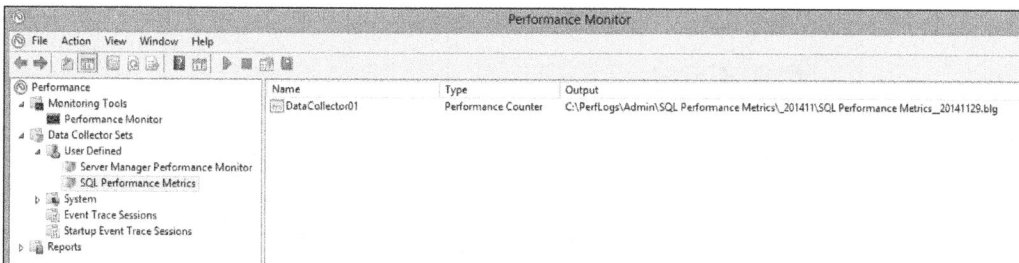

Notice that the folder and filename follows what we specified in the script—plaYearMonth for subdirectory format and plaYearMonth for filename format. If you don't see the file yet, check that the data collector set is started. The file will not appear before then:

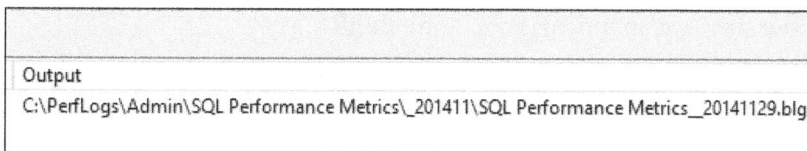

Output
C:\PerfLogs\Admin\SQL Performance Metrics_201411\SQL Performance Metrics__20141129.blg

If you double-click on this entry, a properties window should appear where you can double-check all the entries you provided in your script:

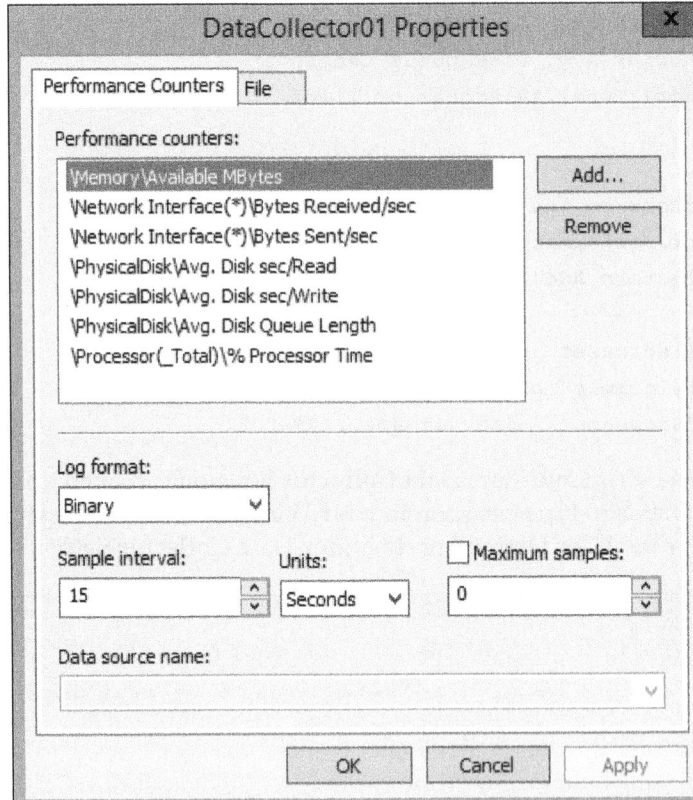

When you are ready to start collecting your data, you can run the following:

```
#asynchronous, don't need to wait for process to end
    $dcs.start($false)
```

The `$false` value parameter just specifies asynchronous, meaning that we don't need to wait for the process to end before we script returns. When you want to stop, you can issue the corresponding `stop()` method.

You can also programmatically schedule when the data collector will run. For each data collector set object, you can use the schedules property and the `CreateSchedule()` method within that. Assuming you've created a variable called `$startdate`, you can use the following snippet to schedule your data collector set:

```
$schedule = $dcs.schedules.CreateSchedule()
$schedule.StartDate = $startdate
```

Alternatively, you can also run these perfmon counters using `logman`, which is a utility that comes with Windows that can run and manage schedules for performance counters and event trace logs. This is the basic syntax for `logman`:

```
logman [create | query | start | stop | delete| update | import |
  export | /?] [options]
```

You can learn more about `logman` at `http://technet.microsoft.com/en-ca/library/cc753820.aspx`.

Summary

We covered a few examples of how you could monitor and automate SQL Server tasks in this chapter. Albeit small, this knowledge should open up a world of possibilities for you when you decide to monitor and automate using PowerShell. These are a few items you could consider monitoring: backup jobs, database connectivity, service pack installations, schema changes, and tracking suspicious logins.

PowerShell would also be great with administrative tasks, such as exporting information to files and managing files (deleting or archiving files older than x number of days for instance).

Remember, however, that PowerShell is still just another tool. There may be better or worse tool options for what you are trying to accomplish. Just make sure that you evaluate the trade-offs and go with the one that offers the most benefit to you or your project/company.

If you choose to stay in the PowerShell path however, you are most likely to be impressed with its capabilities. It's a maturing platform, and more and more Microsoft applications are being released that support cmdlets, which makes PowerShell even more powerful. This is just the beginning of your adventure. So don't be afraid to experiment and push the boundaries of what you can do with PowerShell.

Implementing Reusability with Functions and Modules

We have covered quite a few PowerShell snippets throughout the book. Instead of re-typing these snippets over and over again however, we can start writing and organizing them in a way that makes them reusable. In this appendix, we will explore how to create functions and script modules in PowerShell.

Functions

One way to wrap your script into something reusable and flexible is by converting it into a function. A function, also called a subroutine in other programming languages, is defined as a named group of statements that perform a specific task.

A PowerShell function does exactly that. It wraps lines of code into a single named construct and does a specific task. You can create simple or advanced PowerShell functions.

Simple functions

The simplest function you can create just requires the `function` keyword, the function name, and your code wrapped in curly braces:

```
#----------------------------------------------------#
# simple function skeleton
#----------------------------------------------------#

function <function name>
{
    #your code here
}
```

Here is an example of a very simple function that gets a list of tables for a specific database:

```
#----------------------------------------
# simple function definition
#----------------------------------------
function Get-Tables
{
    Import-Module SQLPS -DisableNameChecking

    $servername = "ROGUE"     # or localhost
    $databasename = "AdventureWorks2014"

    $server = New-Object "Microsoft.SqlServer.Management.Smo.Server" $servername


    $server.Databases[$databasename].Tables
}


#----------------------------------------
# invoke
#----------------------------------------
Get-Tables
```

Notice that this code isn't very different from the code you would write in a regular ad hoc script, except for the function keyword that envelopes the whole code.

> When naming your functions, observe the Noun-Verb convention, and, as much as possible, use only the approved verbs. You can find the approved verbs at http://msdn.microsoft.com/en-us/library/ms714428(v=vs.85).aspx.

Advanced functions

A more flexible, advanced function will incorporate a few more components, including the `CmdletBinding` attribute, parameters with names and options, and comment-based help. Here is an example skeleton that you can use as a reference. Note the embedded comments that describe some of the sections:

```
function <function name>
{
    <#
      comment based help
    #>

    [CmdletBinding()]
    param
      (
        #parameter options, validation, default values
      )

    begin
    {
      #pre-processing
#code executed once, only at the beginning
    }

    process
    {
      #code executed once for each item that
      #is passed to the pipeline

    #use exception handling
    try
    {
    }
    catch
    {
        throw
    }
    finally
    {
    }
```

```
    }

    end
    {
    #post-processing
    #code executed once, before function terminates
    }
}
```

As with any other programming language, it is best to comment and document the code you write. PowerShell supports comment-based help, which means you can use comments to describe the function in more detail.

Comment-based help can be placed as follows:

- At the top of the script, before the function keyword
- At the beginning of the function body
- At the end of the function body

Comment-based help has to follow certain conventions; for example, every topic or keyword must be preceded by a dot. Here are some of the common keywords you are going to find in a comment-based help:

```
<#
.SYNOPSIS
    Synopsis here
.DESCRIPTION
    description here
.PARAMETER parametername
    parameter description here
.EXAMPLE
    Example usage here
.INPUTS
.OUTPUTS
.NOTES
.LINK
#>
```

Once you have incorporated comment-based help in your function definition, you can start using the `Get-Help` cmdlet with your function name to display the help, just as you would with other native PowerShell cmdlets. Learn more about comment-based help at `http://technet.microsoft.com/en-us/library/hh847834.aspx`.

When working with functions, usually you will find the `CmdletBinding` attribute after the function header. The `CmdletBinding` attribute, as per MSDN (`http://msdn.microsoft.com/en-us/library/hh847872.aspx`) is:

> *"... an attribute of functions that makes them operate like compiled cmdlets that are written in C#, and it provides access to features of cmdlets."*

To make functions extensible and flexible, you will have to code it so that it uses parameters. Parameters are values that are passed to the function that the function uses for further processing. As with function definitions, you can make your parameter definitions either simple or more complex. A very simple way of creating parameters is to enclose your parameters in `param()`, and define them simply with a datatype and name:

```
function functionname
{
    param(
      [string]$param1,
      [string]$param2
    )
    #rest of function code here
    #that uses the parameters
}
```

> You can create more complex parameter definitions by specifying different arguments. Some arguments that are supported include `Mandatory`, `Position`, `ParameterSetName`, `ValueFromPipeline`, `HelpMessage`, and `Switch`. You can learn more about advanced parameters at `http://technet.microsoft.com/en-us/library/hh847743.aspx`.

Here is an example of a function that incorporates comment-based help and some of the parameter arguments mentioned just mentioned:

```
function Get-Tables
{
<#
.SYNOPSIS
   Function that retrieves tables from a database
.DESCRIPTION
   Function that retrieves tables from a database
.PARAMETER servername

.PARAMETER databasename
.EXAMPLE
   Get-Tables -servername "Rogue" -databasename "Registration"
.EXAMPLE
   Get-Tables "Rogue" "Registration"
.EXAMPLE
   "Rogue", "Registration" | Get-Tables
.INPUTS
   System.String,System.String
.OUTPUTS
.NOTES
.LINK
#>
   [CmdletBinding()]
   param
   (
     #parameter 1
     [parameter(
        Mandatory=$true,
        ValueFromPipeline=$true,
        ValueFromPipelineByPropertyName=$true,
        HelpMessage='Which server are you using?')]
        [Alias('host')]
        [string]$servername,

     #parameter 2
```

```
    [parameter(
      Mandatory=$true,
      ValueFromPipeline=$true,
      ValueFromPipelineByPropertyName=$true,
      HelpMessage='Which database are you using?')]
      [Alias('database')]
      [string]$databasename


  )


  begin
  {
    Import-Module SQLPS -DisableNameChecking
    $server = New-Object "Microsoft.SqlServer.Management.Smo.Server"
$servername
  }


  process
  {
    try
    {
      $server.Databases[$databasename].Tables
    }
    catch
    {
      Write-Warning $error
    }
    finally
    {
    }
  }


  end
  {
  }
}
```

```
#------------------------------------------
# invoke
#------------------------------------------
"Rogue",  "pubs" | Get-Tables


#------------------------------------------
# get help
#------------------------------------------
Get-Help Get-Tables -full
```

Best practices

Here are some good practices to observe when creating functions:

- Don't try to make your functions do too much. Your functions should do one task and do that one task well.

- Follow the standard naming conventions. Use the approved verbs. Otherwise, warnings will be generated when the unconventionally named functions are used. It might also cause confusion among the other administrators or developers in your team.

- Use the `CmdletBinding` attribute to make the function behave like a native cmdlet.

- Document your code. Use comment-based help.

- Add validation and exception handling to your code. If it encounters error, code it so that it exits gracefully and cleanly.

Ed Wilson, who runs the *Hey, Scripting Guy!* blog posted a best practices series for functions. These blog posts contain golden nuggets of advice and highly recommended reading resources, if you want to improve your PowerShell function-scripting skills:

- PowerShell best practices: simple functions available at `http://blogs.technet.com/b/heyscriptingguy/archive/2014/05/29/powershell-best-practices-simple-functions.aspx`

- PowerShell best practices: advanced functions available at `http://blogs.technet.com/b/heyscriptingguy/archive/2014/05/30/powershell-best-practices-advanced-functions.aspx`

Modules

PowerShell modules are another way to implement reusability in your scripting. A PowerShell module is more extensive than a function because it can contain multiple items like functions, variables, providers, workflows, and so on. Modules can also persist on a disk, and can be referenced or imported by other scripts.

There are four types of modules as of PowerShell V4:

- A *script module* is created from a PowerShell script code.

- A *binary module* is based on a **dynamic linked library (dll)** file.

- A *manifest module* is a module that includes a manifest, which describes what a module contains and how it is processed (visit http://msdn.microsoft.com/en-us/library/dd878337(v=vs.85).aspx).

- A *dynamic module* is one that is not persisted to a disk. These can be created using the New-Module cmdlet.

In this appendix, we are only going to focus on script modules. However, if you are interested in creating the other types of modules, you can refer to http://msdn.microsoft.com/en-us/library/dd878324(v=vs.85).aspx.

Script modules

As I just mentioned, one type of module we can create is called script module. This allows you to create modules purely from your PowerShell script code – either an existing one, or one you're about to write.

The steps to create script modules are as follows:

1. Save your .ps1 file to .psm1.
2. Optionally, create a folder in one of the standard modules folder. This has to have the same name as your module file.
3. Import the module.

Modules, by default, are saved in a few default folders. To see these folders, you can use the environment variable $env:PSModulePath. This returns a semicolon-delimited string. To see each directory in its own line, you can use the split method:

```
($env:PSModulePath -split ";")
```

The following screenshot shows the result I got in my environment:

```
PS C:\> ($env:PSModulePath -split ";")
C:\Users\Administrator.QUERYWORKS\Documents\WindowsPowerShell\Modules
C:\Program Files\WindowsPowerShell\Modules
C:\Windows\system32\WindowsPowerShell\v1.0\Modules\
C:\Program Files (x86)\Microsoft SQL Server\120\Tools\PowerShell\Modules\
```

Here is a simple illustration of how you can convert your script files into a module. Assume we have a file called `Custom.ps1` that contains some PowerShell scripts. Usually, we run this file before we can use the functions inside it. To convert this into a script module, take the following steps:

1. Rename the `Custom.ps1` file to `Custom.psm1`.

2. Create a folder called `Custom` in one of the standard module folders. Let's choose `C:\Windows\system32\WindowsPowerShell\v1.0\Modules`.

3. Save the `Custom.psm1` file in the `Custom` folder:

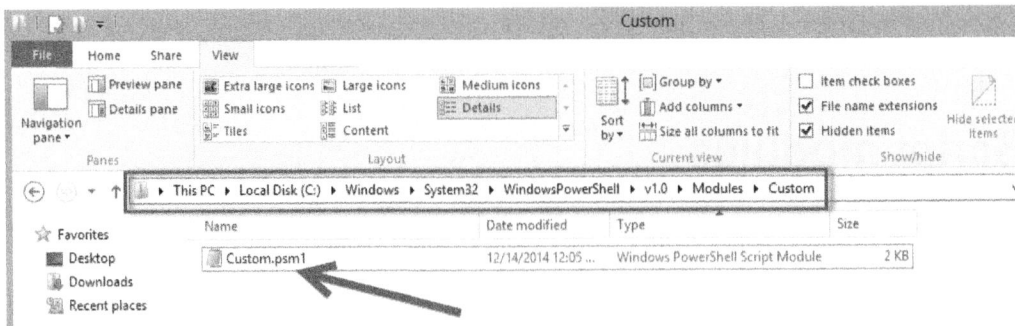

4. Open your PowerShell console or ISE and import the module using the `Import-Module` cmdlet. Recall though that starting from PowerShell V3, module autoloading is supported, meaning that you don't have to explicitly import the module. Once you use the functions in that module, the module is essentially imported (as long as the module is stored in one of the standard folders):

```
PS C:\> Import-Module Custom -Verbose
VERBOSE: Loading module from path 'C:\Windows\system32\WindowsPowerShell\v1.0\Modules\Custom\Custo
m.psm1'.
VERBOSE: Exporting function 'Get-Tables'.
VERBOSE: Importing function 'Get-Tables'.
```

In the preceding screenshot, the `-Verbose` switch was used to show that the `.psm1` file was imported from the `Custom` folder.

5. Test; in other words, use the function inside the module:

```
PS C:\> Get-Tables "Rogue" "pubs"

Schema                          Name                    Created
------                          ----                    -------
dbo                             authors                 9/6/2014 1:58 PM
dbo                             discounts               9/6/2014 1:58 PM
dbo                             employee                9/6/2014 1:58 PM
dbo                             jobs                    9/6/2014 1:58 PM
dbo                             pub_info                9/6/2014 1:58 PM
dbo                             publishers              9/6/2014 1:58 PM
dbo                             roysched                9/6/2014 1:58 PM
dbo                             sales                   9/6/2014 1:58 PM
dbo                             stores                  9/6/2014 1:58 PM
dbo                             titleauthor             9/6/2014 1:58 PM
dbo                             titles                  9/6/2014 1:58 PM
```

Summary

It is considered good practice to wrap scripts that you often use into something more reusable and extensible. Functions and modules are two PowerShell constructs that help you do that. This chapter provided an introduction to creating functions and script modules in PowerShell. You can build up on the basics that you learned from here to create more advanced functions or implement other types of modules.

Index

Thank you for buying
PowerShell for SQL Server Essentials

About Packt Publishing

Packt, pronounced 'packed', published its first book, *Mastering phpMyAdmin for Effective MySQL Management*, in April 2004, and subsequently continued to specialize in publishing highly focused books on specific technologies and solutions.

Our books and publications share the experiences of your fellow IT professionals in adapting and customizing today's systems, applications, and frameworks. Our solution-based books give you the knowledge and power to customize the software and technologies you're using to get the job done. Packt books are more specific and less general than the IT books you have seen in the past. Our unique business model allows us to bring you more focused information, giving you more of what you need to know, and less of what you don't.

Packt is a modern yet unique publishing company that focuses on producing quality, cutting-edge books for communities of developers, administrators, and newbies alike. For more information, please visit our website at www.packtpub.com.

About Packt Enterprise

In 2010, Packt launched two new brands, Packt Enterprise and Packt Open Source, in order to continue its focus on specialization. This book is part of the Packt Enterprise brand, home to books published on enterprise software – software created by major vendors, including (but not limited to) IBM, Microsoft, and Oracle, often for use in other corporations. Its titles will offer information relevant to a range of users of this software, including administrators, developers, architects, and end users.

Writing for Packt

We welcome all inquiries from people who are interested in authoring. Book proposals should be sent to author@packtpub.com. If your book idea is still at an early stage and you would like to discuss it first before writing a formal book proposal, then please contact us; one of our commissioning editors will get in touch with you.

We're not just looking for published authors; if you have strong technical skills but no writing experience, our experienced editors can help you develop a writing career, or simply get some additional reward for your expertise.

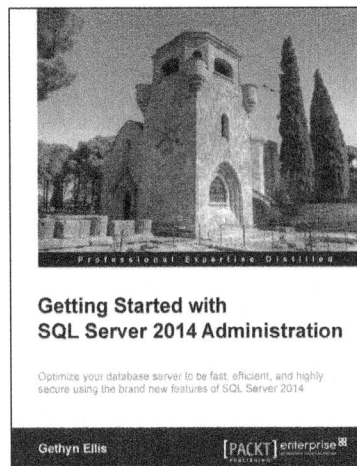

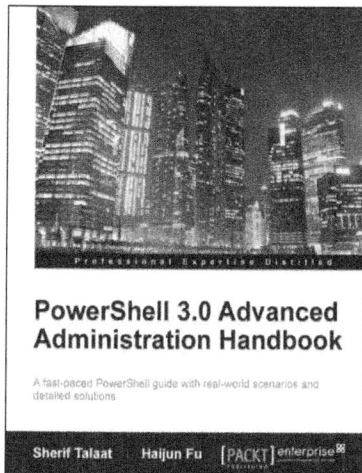

PowerShell 3.0 Advanced Administration Handbook

ISBN: 978-1-84968-642-6   Paperback: 370 pages

A fast-paced PowerShell guide with real-world scenarios and detailed solutions

1. Discover and understand the concept of Windows PowerShell 3.0.

2. Learn the advanced topics and techniques for a professional PowerShell scripting.

3. Explore the secret of building custom PowerShell snap-ins and modules.

4. Take advantage of PowerShell integration capabilities with other technologies for better administration skills.

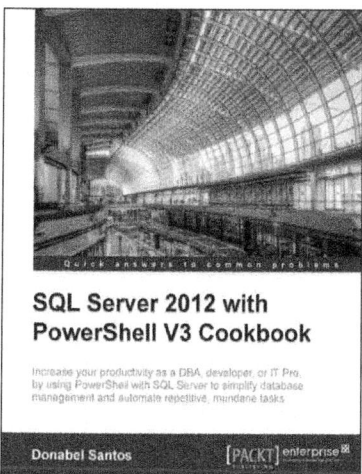

SQL Server 2012 with PowerShell V3 Cookbook

ISBN: 978-1-84968-646-4   Paperback: 634 pages

Increase your productivity as a DBA, developer, or IT Pro, by using PowerShell with SQL Server to simplify database management and automate repetitive, mundane tasks

1. Provides over a hundred practical recipes that utilize PowerShell to automate, integrate and simplify SQL Server tasks.

2. Offers easy to follow, step-by-step guide to getting the most out of SQL Server and PowerShell.

3. Covers numerous guidelines, tips, and explanations on how and when to use PowerShell cmdlets, WMI, SMO, .NET classes or other components.

Please check **www.PacktPub.com** for information on our titles

Lightning Source UK Ltd.
Milton Keynes UK
UKOW05f1652230616

276939UK00014B/238/P

9 781784 391492